Final Honours Thesis of
Martin J. Morris, Department
of Psychology, University of Melbourne.

Comprising one part of the final
assessment for the Degree of
Bachelor of Arts (Hons).

Thesis Supervisor: Professor Alexander
Wearing

Submitted for examination
November 1982.

Effects of Decision Training among
Managers and Professional Staff in
Two Large Organisations

Martin J. Morris
University of Melbourne

Table of Contents

Table of Contents - Continued

Table of Contents - Continued

Abstract

The efficacy of aids to individual decision making has received little or no attention in published psychological literature. A number of untested assertions have been made in recent years concerning the usefulness of training in decomposition techniques as an aid to decision makers. This study examined the effects of such training on groups of managers and senior professional staff in two large organisations. It was expected that subjects trained in a systematic procedure for decomposing decisions would report a more structured approach to information processing in their decision making. Discriminant analysis of six principal factors identified from responses to a Decision Making Questionnaire failed to identify significant differences between trained and untrained subjects. Trained subjects expressed more dissatisfaction with lack of goal clarity in organisational settings. The principal benefit of training was reported as an aid to communication in decision making groups. It was expected that differences would be found between organisations; as one organisation had "institutionalized" such training programs over some years. No significant differences were found between organisations on any of the six factors. 27 trained subjects of both sexes were matched with 27 untrained subjects. Additional data was collected from interviews with each subject. It was concluded that, at their present stage of development, normative theories of decision behaviour do not account for a sufficiently large proportion of variance to be useful as aids to individual judgment and decision making. It was conjectured that social learning theory provides a more useful model of decision behaviour in organisations.

Decision making is defined here in its widest meaning. Human decisions form an interrelated pattern of thought and action. The isolation of a particular decision is a logical impossibility, since every decision creates the conditions for a later set of thoughts and actions leading to further decision behaviour. The process by which individuals reach a point of commitment to a particular course of action is as yet unclear. What is clearly indisputable is the fact that some individuals consistently achieve more successful outcomes from their decision behaviour than others.

Formal attempts to systematically improve decision making behaviour have been developing with increasing momentum since the Second World War, when military demands required decision makers to operate quickly in conditions of complexity, uncertainty and conflict over resources. Since that time, Decision Analysts, as they have come to be called, have developed a range of techniques for aiding decision makers. These decision aids aim to overcome the limitations of human information processing by decomposing the decision task into smaller, more manageable steps.

Summary of Research Aims and Design

The present study examined the effects of
training in the decision aiding procedures formu-
lated by Kepner & Tregoe (1965). Subjects in this
study had received a minimum of thirty-five hours
of training as part of their professional development in two large organisations. The training,
although based on the methodology developed by
Kepner and Tregoe (1965), was adapted to meet the
particular requirements of each organisation.

Interest in decision aiding strategies is
gaining pace, there have been few if any published
results of its usefulness in organisations however.
Since no theory of decision aiding has been formu-
lated, the nature of the research reported here
was exploratory. As in all applied research, the
aim was to establish the usefulness of the procedure
to those for whom it has been proposed to be useful.

Subjects were matched with untrained groups
in each organisation. All subjects completed a
Decision Making Questionnaire, Decision Style
Inventory and assessed various decision related
activities for their relative difficulty. Subjects
were each interviewed by the author to establish
the usefulness of the training in the case of the
trained groups; in the case of the untrained groups

the interviews were designed to gather data on individual perceptions of difficulty in decision making.

Results were analysed using Factor Analytic procedures, Multivariate Analysis of Variance and Hierarchical Cluster Analysis in order to identify differences between trained and untrained groups.

Background to the Development of Decision Aids

Fischhoff (1980), cited in Einhorn and Hogarth (1981) notes that

> like psychotherapy, decision analysis is advocated because the theory is persuasive, because many practitioners are extremely talented and because the alternative seems to be to sink back into the abyss (seat of the pants decision making). (p 81).

Indeed there has been little systematic evaluation of decision aids. The question of their contribution, if any, to the improved quality of decision making has been raised by Einhorn and Hogarth (1981).

The problem of evaluating the effectiveness of decision aids is unlikely to be resolved in the laboratory setting. Ebbesen & Konečni (1980), cited in Einhorn and Hogarth (1981), found that the external validity of decision making research carried out in the laboratory is low. They pointed out that outcomes are affected by context, relevance of alternatives, number of alternatives, concreteness of information, order of presentation and familiarity with the background to the decision. These are but a few of the variables affecting the decision maker faced with a consequential choice in reality.

Janis and Mann (1977) concluded their review of the literature concerning hypothetical decision problems with the statement,

> when people are confronted with a
> consequential choice, they often react in
> an entirely different way than when they
> are confronted with the same cognitive
> problem as a purely hypothetical issue or
> as an intellectual exercise. p 69.

This is best explained by the distinction between the conflict inherent in making judgments and that inherent in taking action. When consequential action is being considered by a decision maker the level of conflict is dependent upon potential losses and gains for the decision maker. These losses and gains can take a variety of forms. Apart from any material loss, the psychological consequences of a poor choice operate as a strong motivating factor.

With a few exceptions, notable among them
the work of Milgram (1974), the laboratory experi-
ment engenders little personal commitment to
conflict inducing action. It is possible to develop
models of decision making behaviour in the laboratory.
The refinement of such models, including cognitive
aids to decision making; and the evlauation of their
usefulness requires an ecologically valid setting.
In view of the limitations of the laboratory, the
efficiency of decision aids must be evaluated in
real decision making environments.

The applied behavioural science of decision
analysis, together with its sister technology,
Knowledge Engineering is growing rapidly alongside
computer technology. At the present time, computer
technology is considerably further advanced than
our capacity to utilize it in aiding decision
makers. The future development of computer aided
decision making holds great technical promise. For
the time being however, man's limited knowledge of
his own cognitive processes remains the obstacle to
rapid evolution of interactive man-machine systems.

At the present time, computer assisted decision
aids are being developed for a limited range of
commercial and medical applications. These aids
depend on the creation of a large and reliable data
base. Their efficiency in comparing incomplete sets

of data with the comprehensive data stored in
the computer, and estimating the probabilities of
conditions existing in the milieu of the limited
data set is being demonstrated. In the commercial
field, such predictive aids are being used in the
geological exploration of oil and mineral deposits.
Medical applications in preventive medicine and
early diagnosis of disease are also being developed
in the technologically advanced nations.

The demand for reliable decision making
information in complex and competitive organisations is increasing. There can be little doubt that
sophisticated interactive decision aiding systems
will be developed, using computer technology that
is becoming relatively inexpensive. These systems
will be developed, with or without a deeper understanding of the cognitive and affective processes
of the human organism.

The extent to which these emerging systems
are congruent with the innate dispositions and
learned decision behaviour of the human organism,
whose lives they will affect, is unknown and
deserves careful study.

Beginning in the United States, after the
Second World War the practice of decision analysis
became increasingly accepted. The origins are not
easily traced. Military exigencies played a part,

as did "commercial" development organisations such as Rand Corporation.

The American universities had, since their beginning, established links with free enterprise. The closer links between universities, military research establishments and free enterprise in the U.S. provided fertile ground upon which the researcher-practitioner in the applied behavioural science of decision analysis could develop. The application of decision analysis as a technique for assisting government and commercial organisations, has become widespread in various forms. Many of the practitioners began their careers as academics; teaching in disciplines related to business, such as economics, applied psychology and computer science.

This brief description is relevant here for two important reasons. The first is specific to the research reported here. The second is more general. The most widely used decision aiding technique in the world was developed by Charles Kepner and Benjamin Tregoe of Princeton N.J. They developed the set of problem solving and decision making procedures described in the Rational Manager, Kepner & Tregoe (1965), after leaving the Rand Corporation. According to their book, Rand Corporation showed no interest in their empirically developed product. They then set about marketing the

product of their ideas, which they continue to do
with some considerable success. According to The
New Rational Manager, Kepner & Tregoe (1981), over
one million people have experienced the training
program. These trained people are employed by
several hundred of the largest corporations and
government agencies around the world. It is the
procedures for problem solving and decision making
developed by Kepner & Tregoe (1965 & 1981), together
with ideas developed independently by the author
and others in Shell Company that formed the training programs in the two organisations under study.

The second and more general reason for describing the commercial development of decision analysis
relates to its continuing locus of interest to
researchers and practitioners. The Decision
Analysis Unit at Brunel University in the U.K. was
established under the leadership of Lawrence Phillips,
himself a Bayesian decision theorist. It is the
author's view that the development of decision theory
will be facilitated by the increasing interaction of
researchers and practitioners. This opinion is
supported by the increasing number of comments in
the decision theoretical literature calling for
evaluation of decision aids. Following their
quotation of Fischhoff (1980), Einhorn and Hogarth
(1981) summarize the position succinctly.

The importance of Fischhoff's analogy is twofold: it raises basic questions regarding the evaluation of decision aids, and it provides some necessary (if not sufficient) motivation to do something about it. p 81.

Although decision aids are far from unitary, they share a common aim. If it were possible in the face of such a complex interelated range of behaviour to isolate a few of what Hogarth (1980) has referred to as "rules of thumb that can be applied with confidence under specified circumstances" p 148, the process of aiding human judgment would have come a long way.

It seems unlikely that a search for comprehensive algorithmic solutions to complex human decision making problems would ever produce results with any generality. The arguments for this view will not be pursued here; they are succinctly summarized by Gauld and Shotter (1977).

As this Century draws to a close, man's technical potency in electronic data processing continues to grow exponentially. Concomitantly, his capability for the collection and processing of decision making data has been enormously expanded. Knowledge of the capacities of human decision makers' judgment and choice has not kept pace with technological advances. Little is known, for example, of the

conditions that make for optimal choices. Thorngate
(1980) has suggested that human motives are often
adapted to the limits of individual cognitive
abilities.

Driver and Mock (1975) found that many decision
makers use less than the amount of readily available
data to make decisions, while continuing to prefer
more. Applied computer technology will increasingly
provide greater availability of decision making
information. Under these conditions, what can be
expected of the human decision maker? Without a
great deal more insight into the cognitive and
affective processes of the human decision maker,
it is difficult to predict the effects of providing
an increasing volume of decision data. Optimal
amounts of data, and the form in which it is
presented are likely to vary widely with individuals.

It has been suggested by Jungermann (1980),
that the application of decision technology, at least
in its present state of development, may be disfunctional for individuals. We may be introducing
complexity to the decision making process and making
it appear harder than it really is. If there is a
threat to human autonomy in the application of
decision technology, it is difficult to elucidate
without a much greater understanding of human decision
making and its meaning and value to the individual.

Dubin in Dunnette (1976), has argued that the role of the practitioner in theory building is an essential and complimentary one to the theorist. The practitioner can contribute most to the theory building enterprise by maintaining the critical appraisal that his contact with the real world entitles him to make.

The human race, at almost all levels of socio-economic development, is becoming a technology dependent species at an accelerating pace. The psychological implications of this symbiotic process have never been more deserving of man's attention. In a review of research findings concerning the effects of information overload on individuals, MacCrimmon and Taylor (1976), concluded that the conceptual structure of individuals is the principal determinant of optimal information load. In complex environments, the conceptual structure of the decision maker appears to influence his effectiveness in coping with the demands of the situation. Internal search processes do not appear to vary with information load. Conceptually abstract decision makers are expected to make better use of available data, while those with more conceptually concrete strategies are expected to continue searching for more information. It is perhaps the conceptually concrete decision maker who continues to prefer more information than he is able to use.

The processes of decision making behaviour at the level of the human organism require careful study in real world contexts.

Benjamin Franklin may not have been the first advocate of what is today called decision analysis. He is however, the most frequently quoted early exponent. A lengthy extract from his letter to the British Scientist Joseph Priestley is reprinted in Janis and Mann (1977) p 149. In his letter, he sets out a simple procedure for dealing with multiple value decisions. The procedure, which he described as a "moral algebra" for making decisions of a complex nature, assumes that each alternative is clearly specified. Franklin summarized the benefits of such a procedure thus.

> And, though the weight of reasons cannot be taken with the precision of algebraic quantities, yet when each is thus considered, separately and comparatively, and the whole lies before me, I think I can judge better, and am less liable to make a rash step, and in fact I have found great advantage from this kind of equation.

Franklin's procedure might be compared with the "Elimination by Aspects" approach described by Tversky (1972). In the former; alternatives are eliminated on the basis of their undesirable features and in the latter, it is claimed, that only alternatives that include selected aspects are considered. The weakness of each lies in the absence of an objective weighting mechanism. Such a mechanism would have the effect of maintaining at least some consistency in judgments.

The Decision Aiding Procedures Developed by

Kepner & Tregoe (1965, 1981)

The procedures for assisting decision makers, developed by Kepner & Tregoe go some way towards overcoming this weakness. They recommend that decision objectives be specified before alternatives are considered in detail. Each objective is assigned a relative value describing its importance to the decision maker. Each alternative is then compared to the objectives singly. A composite set of weighted values is determined for each alternative. This set of values depends on the weight of the objective and the likely performance of each alternative in meeting that particular objective. Following this stage of analysis, those alternatives performing best on the composite set of decision objectives, are examined for features that could weaken their performance. This examination of possible adverse consequences is a critical step in the process recommended by

Kepner and Tregoe.

The decision maker is urged to identify two specific components of such adverse consequences. Firstly the probability of occurrence, and secondly the seriousness of the effects on the decision if they were to occur. Kepner and Tregoe (1981) do not claim that such an analysis will yield solutions approaching the ideal. They maintain that a careful analysis provides "a realistic platform from which to build improvements and make rational choices. p 120.

Where alternatives are not immediately apparent, Kepner & Tregoe have observed managers to be more concerned with generating them, than with specifying decision objectives. The decision maker beginning with a well defined set of objectives has the advantage of a logical & consistent structure within which creative solutions may be developed. They also argued that such a structure enables the earlier recognition of fruitful ideas. Inadequate methods of evaluation are claimed to stifle creativity by psychologically inhibiting the contributions of those decision makers in subordinate positions of power.

The ease with which a technique for organising relevant decision making information may be mastered, and thus provide feedback on its potential usefulness is an important consideration. This is true not only

for teachers and students of decision making,
but for those who may not be a party directly to
the decision but are nonetheless affected by it.
It is a frequent observation, made by those working in organisations, that a decision is worthless
until its outcome can be evaluated. This is a
position that would undoubtedly be challenged by
Kepner and Tregoe.

Formal Decision Analysis

Winterfeldt (1980) has identified the most
important step in decision analysis as being the
structuring of the decision problem into a manageable format. He admits that this is an art "left to
the intuition and craftsmanship of the individual
analyst." p 71. A well structured decision problem
is one in which the present position, desired outcome and the transformation process of decision
making are clear in the mind of the decision maker.
Most important decisions are by definition, ill
structured. The processes by which the decision
problem may be transformed into a set of well
defined elements, relationships and procedures are
the concern of decision analysts.

Decision analysts are generally not concerned
with teaching procedures of information processing
useful to decision makers. Such procedures are an

aid to decision making, but not a substitute for formal decision analysis. In formal decision analysis, the client and the decision analyst work together on the development of the best possible solution to the client's particular problem. In the process the client learns techniques, that may be transferable to other decision problems. It is the individual problem centred relationship that exists between decision analyst and client, which sets decision analysis apart from the type of decision aid developed by Kepner and Tregoe (1965). The latter was the concern of this study. The research question of interest concerns the usefulness of training in the procedures for systematic decomposition of decisions recommended by Kepner and Tregoe (1965).

In designing this study it was considered appropriate to take the widest possible view of "use value". It is not unusual to discover in the course of inquiry such as this, unintended consequences of training and unexpected outcomes. It was hoped that in addition to exploring several general research questions, information would be gathered which would permit the formulation of more specific research hypotheses.

Strategies for Decision Aiding

Hammond, McCelland and Mumpower (1980) have

defined two separate forms of decision aiding
strategies. The first

> deals with probabilities and utilities
> and address themselves to the results of
> inductive knowing, that is, to the cognitive
> state of an individual subsequent to the
> acquisitiion of knowledge.   p 105.

The second type are judgment aids, and address
themselves to the sources of probabilities and
utilities. The distinction between the purposes
of each is that the former is concerned with deciding and the latter with the more conative process
of "knowing". It is with the usefulness of the
former that this study is concerned.

Slovic Fischhoff and Lichtenstein (1977)
concluded that decomposing the decision task into
smaller more manageable components was a constructive response to the problem of information overload.
They cite several studies that have shown decomposition techniques to improve judgment in decision
making tasks in the laboratory setting. Tversky
(1972) pointed out that decision makers have less
confidence in the judgments they make intuitively,
than in their decisions. It follows from this,
that any decision aid that successfully improves
confidence in the judgments which are a subset of
the decision process, should improve the overall

quality of individual decisions. By recombining
the decomposed structure of the decision to form
a judgment in which important details have not been
overlooked, the decision maker should, at least on
average, make decisions with closer to optimal
outcomes.

Hogarth (1980) in a comprehensive and very
readable review of decision theory and its possible
practical applications, offers a number of reasons
for optimism. He states that, in his view, intuition
can not only be studied, but educated. In other
words he believes the methods used by people to
manipulate the knowledge they have, and collect
further information, can be modified to advantage.
He concedes that decision analysis by decomposition
is no panacea, however he argues for its superiority
over methods. Judgments, he argues are "the result
of interaction between the structure of tasks and
the nature of the human information processing system."
p 14.

Brunswik (1956) cited in Hammond et al (1980)
asserted that judgments are made in an invironment
that is perceived by decision makers as probabilistic.
It is the complexity of the individual perception
of the environment that determines the degree of
uncertainty experienced by the organism. Any

decision aiding procedure that assists in a more complete perception of the environment, by systematically seeking out and evaluating relevant data, should contribute to a reduction in subjectively perceived uncertainty.

Certainly the causal texture of environments is not static and unchanging. However the organism is able to respond to the environment, and by doing so in an adaptive fashion, reduce the level of uncertainty experienced. What is meant here by adaptive behaviour in conditions of perceived uncertainty, is that behaviour, which accurately revises existing hypotheses about causal relationships in the world. The decision aid developed by Kepner and Tregoe (1965) was designed specifically to encourage decision makers to systematically and continuously revise existing hypotheses concerning causal relationships in their decision environment.

In an unchanging environment, human decision makers would have little need for such revisions. Probably as a result of greater environmental change than at any previous time, unaided human judgment has become the subject of much attention by a wide range of disciplines. Hogarth (1980) asserted that the frequency of important judgments required of the members of complex socio-technical

systems is increasing. In spite of his optimism,
Hogarth makes only cautious claims for the ability
of existing decision aids. If decision makers
develop their habitual ability to ask critical and
relevant questions, systematically and persistently,
the evidence is claimed by Hogarth, to support
improved decision behaviour. In particular he notes
that a trained decision maker is likely to react
more adaptively when under stress.

The principal difference between the approach
to decision aiding recommended by Hogarth (1980)
and the procedures recommended by Kepner and Tregoe
(1965, 1981), lies in the methodological treatment
of uncertainty. Hogarth acknowledges, not only that
uncertainty must be reckoned with, he outlines some
procedures for assessing it systematically. He also
counsels decision makers on the probabilistic nature
of decision making, pointing out the need for acceptance of this fact. Kepner and Tregoe on the other
hand adopt a much more circumscribed approach to
uncertainty. Their method confines itself largely
to what Hammond et al (1980) referred to as the
cognitive state of the individual subsequent to the
acquisition of knowledge. No mention of the systematic biases, to which decision makers are supposedly
prone, is made by Kepner and Tregoe (1981). Their

method relies then, on systematic collection and organisation of decision making information. They sum up their position as follows:

> The process does not guarantee that perfect decisions will be made every time. Given human fallibility and the usual inadequacy of available information, there will always be errors. At the very least, however, the process of Decision Analysis enables the manager to reduce the incidence of errors by providing a systematic framework for evaluating alternatives. p 102.

Research Evidence Suggesting Systematic Biases in Human Judgment

Hogarth (1980, Chap. 9) reported four main characteristics of judgmental tasks leading to bias. These are summarized as (a) task complexity, (b) procedural uncertainty, (c) psychological regret, (d) emotional stress. He observed that the bulk of processing biases noted in the lterature result from,

> (1) Task variables, (2) unwillingness to expend mental effort, and (3) inconsistency in applying a judgmental rule. p 163.

The last of these was reported to be the major source of processing bias, and the most difficult to diagnose and correct. He admitted that the

tools we have for decision aiding, lack the facility
to capture the essence of important problems.

The nature and complexity of decisions that
are required in today's fast changing world demand
that good judgment be learned with minimal feedback.
Bogart (1980) suggested that biases in decision
heuristics may be best compensated for by improving,
not only feedback in living systems, but also by
paying attention to mechanisms of "feedforward"
and "feedwithin". Attention to these functional
mechanisms of living open systems, is a necessary
condition for optimal health and functioning. Feedback, he argues, operates to correct errors in
behaviour only after an error has been committed
and subsequently detected. The decision aiding
procedures recommended by Kepner and Tregoe (1965,
1981) aim at facilitating the application of
consistent judgmental rules. By clarifying decision
objectives and their relative importance to the
decision maker, it has been argued that inconsistency and decision conflict are reduced. The
decision maker becomes a more active agent, resistant to irrelevant feedback, and therefore less
susceptible to psychologically disabling uncertainty.

An important obstacle to effective individual
decision making is the widespread tendency to
overgeneralise to conclusions based on unwarranted

assumptions concerning previous experiences.
Kahneman and Tversky (1972) found this effect to be
pervasive among decision makers. This mental
strategy of arriving at conclusions by the degree
of similarity between events has been named the
"representativeness heuristic" by Kahneman & Tversky
(1972). Tversky & Kahneman (1974) found that many
of the heuristics used by decision makers, lead to
biases of judgment. The "representativeness
heuristic" although useful in routine decisions,
where there are no deviations from the expected
pattern of relationships, can lead to serious
errors in novel and complex decision environments.

One of the strengths claimed for the decision
aiding procedures advocated by Kepner & Tregoe, is
that their systematic application results in a
lowering in the tendency to jump to premature
conclusions. The consequences of such premature
hypothesis formation, has been shown by Tversky
and Kahneman (1977) to result in the decision
maker seeking confirming evidence for it, and
ignoring data that may be contradictory to the
hypothesis.

From a procedural point of view, the structure
recommended for evaluating decision alternatives
by Kepner and Tregoe (1981), Keeney & Raiffa (1976)
and Janis and Mann (1977) are very similar.

Evaluating decision alternatives and the potential
risks associated with each, is a small part of the
process of decision making however. There are
earlier and later steps of critical importance.
The prerequisite to any decision activity, is the
decision maker's appraisal of his present course of
action. If neither challenge nor opportunity
provides motivation to change, the decision maker
will remain in what Janis and Mann (1977) have
described as "unconflicted adherence" to the present
course. The threshold of motivation to change is
highly variable according to Janis and Mann. What
constitutes a threat or an opportunity for one
person, may arouse little psychological conflict in
another. Even when such opportunities or threats
are perceived, they may result in a wide range of
behavioural response. This response may range from
defensive avoidance to hypervigilance according to
the model proposed by Janis and Mann.

Human judgment in probability estimation has
been shown to be fallible under certain conditions.
Hogarth (1980) has provided a lucid and comprehensive review of recent research findings concerning
the sources of error in probability and relability
estimation. It is beyond the scope of this study to
describe all of these in detail; from time to time

individual research findings will be referred to however. The extent to which they are consistently powerful enough to be a significant biasing influence on real world decisions remains an open question.

Kahneman and Tversky (1982) have suggested that our perception of reality is governed in part by our imagination. Our imagination appears to be governed by rules, "and the rules of imagination affect our experience of reality by controlling the alternatives to which it is compared" p 141. They concluded that departures from objectivity in judgment tend to follow regular patterns. These patterns were described mathematically. In general, sure gains are preferred to gambles with a potentially higher reward. The psychological regret associated with failures to take action is generally less intense than that experienced following the failure of an action. Anticipation of regret is likely to result in inertia or cautious decision behaviour rather than an attempt to find a novel solution. The psychological relationship between anticipatory regret and defensive avoidance was not discussed by Kahneman and Tversky. It appears to be an important psychological determinant of decision behaviour. It was explored in this study in relationship to the training in decision making procedures received by each subject.

The final cognitive stage in the decision sequence, made before and during preliminary planning activity, is that concerned with commitment. This is perhaps the most critical and certainly the most contentious stage in decision making. Before it has occurred, the decision can only be viewed as tentative. Prior to arriving at the stage of commitment to a new course of action, the decision maker must come to terms with giving up his previous position. In this sense, every decision involves yielding one course of action in favour of one that is estimated to provide something of greater value.

Joseph Priestley, the British scientist previously mentioned, was perhaps in a decision conflict concerning a major commitment, when he sought the advice of Benjamin Franklin. According to Kuhn (1962),

> Only much later and in part through an
> accident did he renounce the standard pro-
> cedure and try mixing nitric oxide with his
> gas in other proportions. His commitment
> to the original test procedure - a procedure
> sanctioned by much previous experience - had
> been simultaneously a commitment to the non-
> existence of gases that could behave as
> oxygen did.   p 60.

This vivid example illustrates the durability of
this thing called commitment. Decision makers do
not give up existing courses of action easily,
when they have performed satisfactorily in the past.
To do so necessarily involves a degree of risk.
The study of consequential human decision making
is in large part, the study of commitment. To
expect a decision maker to change his habitual
decision making behaviour, is to seek a major
departure from a previous commitment. The exponents
of a more rational procedure will be required to
demonstrate its superior validity before any decision
maker will consider commitment to a new method.

Einhorn & Hogarth (1981) suggested that
decision makers' task representation may be a
considerably more significant factor in defining
errors of judgment than the rules they use within
their own task representation. They point out that
seemingly minor changes in a task affect the context
in which it is to be performed; and thereby the
judgments made concerning it. If it can be demonstrated that aids to human judgment assist in
stabilising and clarifying the task, in the mind of
the decision maker, they will have proved their
worth. It may well be the case that the application
of a systematic and communicable procedure assists
in the resolution of differing task perceptions
between decision makers and no more than that. This

has been one of the observable results of training
in decision making procedures in the author's
experience.

Subjective Impressions of Decision Training

In the period immediately following training
in decision making procedures, for usually one month
or so, decision makers are clearly making a real
effort to be more systematic in their procedures.
As time passes, individual differences in the application of the procedures learned in the training
program, become more identifiable. It is not clear
however whether these apparent differences are due
to training alone; interaction with other decision
makers in the organisation; experiential differences
immediately following the training, acting to reinforce or extinguish the learning; or in fact,
whether the apparent surface behaviour change is
indicative of any real change. It has been the
author's experience that some individuals find the
decision structuring procedures recommended by
Kepner and Tregoe (1965, 1981) more acceptable and
easier to integrate into their existing procedures.

The reasons for this apparent difference are
not clear. Conventional training evaluation procedures have typically indicated a high degree of
acceptance by trainees. Such evaluation procedures
are invariably carried out immediately after the

training. An evaluation was conducted by the
Training Department of Australia Post during the
three months following the pilot training program
carried out by the author in November and December
1980. The results of the post course evaluation
showed a very positive acceptance of the decision
procedures recommended by Kepner & Tregoe (1965).
Thirty five of the thirty nine trainees completed
evaluation forms anonymously. Seventy four percent
of these trainees reported the training to be of
considerable value. Twenty six percent reported
"medium value", and no trainee who completed an
evaluation, thought the procedures would be of
little value. (A copy of the Australia Post training evaluation appears as Appendix A to this study).

With such a positive acceptance of the
procedures, it might reasonably be expected that
modifications to decision behaviour among trained
personnel would take place. The present study
attempted to identify the changes that had taken
place, if any, and establish the extent to which
such changes persist over time.

The difficulty faced by any trainer inside
an organisation begins the moment any serious
attempt at evaluation begins. The reasons are
many. Some are more obvious than others. Firstly,
the trainer is biased. How could he not be?

It was he who made the first investment psychologically in the training and its surface validity. He was pursuaded that such training was of value. From that time onward, at least for as long as he is actively involved as a trainer, he has a tendency to selectively attend to reinforcing stimuli. There are many further obstacles to the reliable measurement of learning. It is not only difficult to elicit reliable data on the extent of learning without contaminating the objectivity of the evaluation; it is also hard to estimate how much of the learning is actually used. It is not surprising therefore that decision theorists, practitioners of decision analysis, and trainers who attempt to confront the issues in an unbiased way, view training in decision aiding with a mixture of caution and optimism.

Conflict and Emotion in Decision Making

The nature of decision problems is highly variable in terms of the demands placed upon the decision maker. Decision makers' perceptions of demands from the situation are also a critical factor in determining level of arousal, emotion and attention. Toda (1980) examines the functional value of emotion in decision making and argues that decision makers cannot afford to treat emotions, positive or negative, as mere inconvenient noise in the system. His conception of the higher cognitive functions being an evolutionary supplement to, but not a replacement of, the emotional decision system has important implications for decision aiding. As an essentially anticipatory system it may well play a greater role in cognitive dissonance than we creatures of consciousness care to admit. The rationality of decomposition techniques and the decision routines they advocate are consistent with normative decision theory. Furthermore they are difficult to confound by any process of analytical logic. By definition, therefore they demand acceptance by "rational" creatures. If Toda's hypothesis is true, our positioning of the emotional decision system in relation to our cognitive functioning should be taken into account when designing any systematic aid to human judgment.

Janis and Mann (1977) have recognised the central role of cognitive conflict in decision making. They cite studies by Hackman (1974) and Hackman & Morris (1975) who concluded that people generally have poor planning skills in obtaining, assimilating and applying decision making information. The evidence summarized by Janis and Mann concerning attempts to improve problem solving and decision making procedures is equivocal. Earlier studies cited by Janis and Mann including Maier, (1963),

Shure et al, (1962) and Varela (1971) found that
training resulted in some temporary improvement
with little or no lasting effect on behaviour.
Janis and Mann refer to "a few pertinent studies
showing promising results". p 371. They do
not give details of these studies however. The
evidence presented by Janis and Mann in support
of the specific adverse effects of psychological
stress on the cognitive processes of problem solving
and decision making is powerful. They identify five
basic patterns of coping behaviour, four of which
they describe in their theory, as being disfunctional to vigilant information processing. The
consequences of poor vigilance in decision making
attributable to each of the disfunctional coping
strategies is described in terms of its likely
effects on decision outcomes.

When a decision maker is faced with a
consequential choice, one factor determining his
behaviour according to the theory, is the manner
in which he normally copes. Since decisions are
presumably perceptually graduated in terms of their
seriousness and urgency for the decision maker, it
would be reasonable to expect individuals to display
consistent and identifiable decision making styles
based on their innate structure and learning history.

Janis and Mann emphasize that their model is concerned only with behaviour in decisions of a consequential nature. The evidence for inconsistency between behaviour in hypothetical situations and real consequentive settings is reviewed on page 69 in Janis & Mann (1977).

Individual Differences in Information Processing Style

It was conjectured that individual decision makers develop characteristic information processing styles. It is suggested here that these information processing styles form part of the habitual problem solving and decision making behaviour of individuals. It was further conjectured that individual decision makers would exhibit a dominant and identifiable style of information processing. Information processing style is defined here as an habitual methodology for seeking and organising data for decision making. Such a dominant style may well be indicative of the sort of strategy used by the individual to cope with situations of complexity and uncertainty. It was not the intention to elucidate the relative effectiveness of each, since this would require value judgments far beyond the scope of this inquiry. The purpose of attempting the identification of differing information processing styles, was to examine the relationship between them and outcomes of training in decision procedures.

Individuals vary in their ability and willingness to integrate such training into their existing decision procedures. It may be the case that the procedures are useful only for some decision makers. If this can be shown to be the case, and the reasons explained, it may suggest useful modifications to decision aiding procedures.

In a study of individual differences in leader decision making, Hill and Schmitt (1977) found interpretable individual differences in decision strategy. Although situational differences accounted for four times as much variance, they found decision makers used only a small number of problem attributes in their decision making, frequently as few as two or three.

The information processing styles developed for this study were based on the findings of Janis and Mann (1977), Driver & Mock (1975) and Kahneman and Tversky (1972). The author's observations of decision makers, both in training and in demanding decision making roles in organisational settings also contributed to their formulation.

Driver & Mock (1975) point to the proliferation of information systems design strategies since the introduction of commercial electronic data processing. They assert that individuals and groups, as systems, develop different information processing strategies. This assertion is based on the assumption that, while people may be unique, and differ in individual cognition, there exist identifiable categories of people with similar thought processes. They postulated that differences in individual information processing strategies are best explained by the individual learning within the context of an organisation. In the same way, organisational differences are assumed to have been learned. Mock, Estrin & Vasarhelyi (1972), cited in Driver and Mock (1975) investigated decision style in a study of behaviour in business games. They found that decision style explained variance in learning patterns and information value.

Learning, related to human information processing in organisations, possibly occurs as a unique way of combining the information processing capacity of the group to meet the needs of its members. Mackinnon & Wearing (1980) have suggested an alternative hypothesis: that complex organisational systems have developed as part of the evolution of the species. This proposition is compatible with the general evolutionary tendency to complexity of the organism. Taken to its logical conclusion, this line of thought suggests that organisms and systems maintain some degree of evolutionary homeostasis between them. This homeostasis is arguably not in evidence at the present time. If one considers evolution to be progressing hierarchically as Toda (1980) and Simon (1969) cited in Mackinnon & Wearing suggest, the former hypothesis appears in need of integration into a theory of living organisms and systems.

Individuals have been found to differ in their tolerance for ambiguity and the degree to which they seek complexity. Whereas some people appear to consistently seek uncertainty and manipulate ambiguity with ease, Driver and Mock (1975) report that others will go to extremes, including conspicuous self deception to avoid it. They report that decision makers frequently continue to prefer more data than they can possibly process. Driver (1970) cited in Driver & Mock (1975), developed a Decision Style Theory with the aim of facilitating the design of information systems more closely matching the needs of decision makers in the context of stable organisations. His findings in the 1975 study referred to above are broadly compatible with Mackinnon and Wearing's (1980) later conclusions concerning heuristic capacity for the reduction of complexity. Driver and Mock found inconsistency in their model of types of decision makers. Contrary to their expectations, they found people who would normally be

expected to spend time considering a wide range
of options and planning a high quality solution, were
in fact not only faster than expected, but continued
to perform under pressure with no decrement in results.
They concluded that early formulation of decision
rules facilitated the superior performance of this
group in a stable environment. In contrast, those
subjects with a tendency to arrive at conclusions
quickly, performed very poorly as a result of information overload in the task environment. These were
the subjects who normally relied on fewer criteria
to make decisions. Their behaviour pattern, as outlined by Driver and Mock was typical of that described
by Newell & Simon (1972) as "satisfycing".

The Value of Decomposition in Decision Aiding

Decision Analysis is based on the premise that
human decision makers are innately equipped with a
greater capability to detect, store and retrieve
information than that which they possess for aggregation of the same data to form a reliable inference.
Decision aids that rely on the method of decomposing
tasks, rely on the same premise.

Hogarth (1980) pointed out that information
can be accessed from two sources. Firstly from
memory and secondly from the task environment. The
relative salience of information can be a variable
function of both sources. Given that memory, past

experience, intelligence and other abilities and
aptitudes are relatively fixed in the short term;
the decision maker may influence structure of the
task environment by his methods of information collection and organisation. Kepner and Tregoe (1965,
1981) argued that decision makers can be taught
efficient and reliable information collection and
manipulation, within their intellectual capacity,
aided only by pencil and paper. Assuming this to be
the case, decision makers should be able to make
more effective use of the fixed intellectual assets
they possess.

To be useful to the decision maker in the
long term, a decision aid must produce noticeably
better results. If it does not, the decision maker
has no incentive to change his customary patterns
of behaviour when confronted with a decision problem.
Part of the cost of using a decision aid is the time
and effort required to acquire skills in its use.
Unless the aid shows early signs of yielding some
return on the material and psychological investment
made in its acquisition it will not be used. To use
such a procedure, however compelling its appeal in
terms of formal rationality, would be a waste of time
and energy. A rational system of decision making,
with the objective of maximising the benefit of outcomes for the decision maker, while minimising risks,

has great appeal for economic reasons alone. It is
not surprising therefore that decision aiding
techniques have been taken up in various forms by
commercial organisations.

MacCrimmon (1968), cited in MacCrimmon and
Taylor (1976), found that executive decision makers
frequently violated the axioms of a decision strategy
aimed at optimising decision outcomes. When this
was pointed out to them, they explained their behaviour
as a mistake to be rectified in future decisions.
It is such apparent inconsistency that the process
of decision aiding attempts to reduce by systematic
decomposition of the task into a sequence of smaller
operations. Each of these operations is assumed to be
represented in the normally unaided decision process.
Errors and inconsistencies, together with suboptimal
decision outcomes in general are attributed to failure
in the decision maker's normally unaided process.
Failure, that is, to adequately structure the decision
problems.

Simon (1976) has expressed the view that man
fails to optimise decision outcomes because he does
not have the wit to do so. Simon maintains that many
of the failures of human information processing may be
mitigated by improving procedures for rational choice.
In Simon's view, learning theories account for the
observed behaviour of decision makers, rather better
than do the theories of rational behaviour.

There is a great deal more to being rational
than merely being logical. Logicality has formal
properties capable of precise mathematical definition.
Rationality on the other hand is related to logicality
only in a formal sense. Definitions of a substantive
rationality are broad and multifaceted, extending
well beyond logicality into the subjective realms
of realism and morality. Decision aids to human
judgment can be concerned with procedural rationality
only in the formal sense. Concerned that is, with
internal consistency and not with the values of the
decision maker. As Simon (1965) observed,

> All these aids to human thinking and many
> others were devised without understanding
> the process they aided - the thought
> itself. p 92.

Janis and Mann (1977) have reviewed the
evidence that decision makers hold conflicting values
over some aspects of their important decisions. A
decision aid requiring precision in the specification
of objectives and alternative courses of action, could
be expected to clarify such conflicts by bringing
them into sharper focus. Ultimately the decision
maker is obliged to make a choice however. In the
process of considering a wider range of alternatives;
and as a result of adopting a more systematic search
for relevant information, the decision maker is
expected to be in a position to make superior choices.

No claim is made that the decision maker will be
capable of superior judgment on all occasions however.
The claims for the benefits of decision aids are
based mainly on the value of improved search and
appraisal of relevant data. If such systematic
procedures are learned and subsequently applied,
the outcomes of decisions are expected to reflect a
more fully integrated use of the decision makers'
past experience and reasoning ability. For these
reasons, the average performance of decisions is
expected to be improved.

Hammond, McClelland and Mumpower (1980)
have summarized the theoretical underpinning of
judgment decomposition. They point out the critical
importance of the attributes that are selected for
decomposition. Each of the approaches they have
reviewed, stresses this importance. They comment:

> All the approaches insist upon attribute
> elicitation, but give little instruction
> about how it should be done: the
> elicitation process is left as an art; one
> of the "tricks of the trade".   p 159.

The process of eliciting a decision maker's
utilities and the relative weighting of these requires
a prescriptive model. MacCrimmon and Taylor (1976)
point out that such a prescriptive model must be
founded in actual behaviour. No prescriptive model
could expect to be either simple or universally

applicable since

>The type of decision problem, the nature
>of the decision environment, and the
>current state of the decision maker dictate
>the strategy required for a solution.   p 1399.

Tversky & Sattath (1979) have concluded that individual choice behaviour is sufficiently variable that attempts to model it can be at best incomplete.

The decomposition process attempts to express the overall value of each decision alternative as a function of the scale values of each of its components.

Armstrong, Denniston and Gordon (1975) found that people can make better judgments when they use the principle of decomposition. They found that judgment was enhanced when the subject provided the data and a computer analysed it. Self analysed decomposition was poorer than that analysed by a computer, but not appreciably so. Aschenbrenner, Jaus and Villani (1980) in a study of students career choice, found subjects' capacity for processing information was almost doubled. The effect apparently persisted over time. In view of the importance of the choice to the subjects, this finding requires further validation. Humphreys and McFadden (1980) have pointed out that the essence of successful decision aiding lies in assisting the decision maker in structuring the problem. They state that it may be that the efficacy of decision aids comes from structuring tasks so that the nature of one's goals is clarified. p 60.

MacCrimmon (1974) has observed a number of suboptimal information processing strategies occurring in real decision making situations. These include, collecting too much information, communicating redundant information and organising decision teams that were unnecessarily large for the task. The effects on decision outcomes of the behaviours observed by MacCrimmon can at best be speculative. Tversky and Kahneman (1977) observed a tendency for people to compound causal data and average data that was not causally related to the immediate problem. The effect of this tendency, if it operates in decision making groups, is likely to result in underestimation of the value of important information merely because it is not immediately causally connected to the problem under review. The effect of such a tendency is likely to have particularly strong impact on strategic decisions, which by their nature are usually made in relatively illstructured environments.

Pitz, Sachs and Heerboth (1980) found that decision makers produced a wider range of alternatives when decision objectives were examined singly. This result may be explained, at least in part, by the results obtained by Tversky & Kahneman (1977). When

decision makers considered each objective in isolation, they were perhaps less constrained by the
tendency to think causally, and therefore produced
a wider range of options. Pitz, Sachs and Heerboth
concluded that the greatest contribution made by
decision aiding is the assistance provided to the
decision maker in recognising alternatives that would
not otherwise have been considered.

Gibson and Nicol (1964) cited in MacCrimmon
& Taylor (1976) found that decisions made, using
more information, were more resistant to change. This
suggests that procedures for eliciting a clear
formulation of decision objectives, a wide range of
alternatives, the assessment of potential risks and
benefits of each, are likely to produce useful and
durable decision choices. In the process of using
such procedures, previously ill structured decision
problems may be progressively transformed to the
point where all the conditions for structure are
improved. Each of these conditions, defined as:
familiarity with the initial state, desired state,
and the transformations necessary for proceding with
information processing, is partly responsible for
the level of the decision makers' motivation to resolve
the decision problem. If the decision aiding process
improves the decision makers' willingness to tackle
problems which are initially ill structured, it

would possibly enhance what Janis and Mann (1977) have referred to as vigilant decision making. This would be true if Hogarth (1980) is correct in his assertion that trained decision makers are likely to respond more appropriately under stress.

Potential Disadvantages of Decision Aiding

Jungermann (1980) has pointed out:

There is a danger that we are making decisions seem more complicated and, thus, less controllable by offering decision aiding systems.   p 22.

He later states, that formal teaching of decision making procedures is only one of several potentially useful strategies.   Another, possibly more effective, would be to give help to young people as part of their education.   He suggests development of tolerance for ambiguity and uncertainty: cognitive flexibility and awareness of the biases that affect judgment and hinder learning from experience.

Brehmer (1980) cites Fischhoff and Slovic (1978) who showed that even very limited experience led to highly unwarranted confidence when people thought they had a good decision rule.   Fischhoff & Slovic concluded that people generally have too much confidence in their decision rules.   Brehmer wondered whether it was either appropriate or practical to teach strategies of decision making based on notions

of chance and probability. Since the work of Piaget
and Inhelder (1974) has shown that these cognitive
facilities are not highly developed until the formal
operations stage is well advanced, such strategies
would be inappropriate for young people. Ginsberg
& Opper (1979) pose the question: "Are the formal
operations universal?" p 201. They concluded that
this is far from being the case, even among adults,
many of whom use formal operations in a very limited
way.

Jungermann (1980) recommended that decision
aids be kept as technically simple as possible when
they are to be taught to people without training and
experience in the application of quantitative analytic
techniques. He urged care in the choice of decision
rules for decision aiding techniques. To be useful,
the rules adopted should be a balanced compromise
between the requirements of typical decision problems
and the characteristics of potential users. As yet,
he states, there are no evaluation studies of the
decision aids developed outside the framework of
decision theory. Assumptions concerning the extent
to which it is appropriate to decompose decision
problems, under varying conditions, have also to be
studied. The need also exists for empirical investigation of self administered and counsellor aided
strategies. He reviews the difficulties in obtaining

reliable data in such empirical studies. Each
of the research designs suggested has its own
limitations. It is a question of choosing the
most appropriate method or combination of methods,
depending on the opportunities presented in the
research ínvironment.

Decision Making in Organisations

Each decision that is made in conditions of
complexity or uncertainty is a function of the human
information processor and the environmental variables
operating on him; before, during and after the decision
is made. Norman (1976) has observed that information
processing is becoming the study of the human. This
is increasingly true for a wider range of disciplines.

Bell (1979) cited in Phillips (1980) has
observed; not only are we moving into a post
industrial world, "but for the first time, innovation
and change derive from the codification of theoretical
knowledge". p 248. Phillips maintains that the
organisational implementation of intellectual tech-
nologies, such as decision analysis, depends more than
anything else on the structure of the organisation.

Organisations that have the greatest facility
for lateral communication are the most likely to
integrate an intellectual technology. The same
organisations are more likely to facilitate individual
effectiveness in coping with uncertainty. The more

hierarchical the organisation structure, and the more centrally controlled are its information sources the less likely it will be to function well in conditions of uncertainty. He admits that the evidence for this proposition is meagre and requires further investigation. He cites Harrison (1977) who found resistance to formal Decision Analysis among senior management in a study of thirty two companies using computer methods of planning. Their objections centred on the subjective nature of probability assessments in strategic decision making, and the difficulty in obtaining agreement on them.

Galbraith (1973) has argued that increased uncertainty creates more exceptions to established rules and procedures in the organisation. The result is a higher demand on decision makers at all levels in the organisation; particularly those in policy making positions.

Ungson, Braunstein & Hall (1981) in a review of information processing research, conclude that in order to obtain a better understanding of the effects of uncertainty in organisations it will be necessary to develop more powerful simulation models. Such models offer the best possibility for studying behaviour in ill structured decision problems over time. They suggested combined simulation - field research in order to trace the variables affecting such decision making.

Thus it may be possible to capture what
we think are the essential realities of
the problem and the organisational decision-
making process in the simulation studies.
p 129.

A reliable and useful prescriptive model of
problem solving and decision making based on sound
theoretical principles is far from complete. In the
meantime there are many indications in the experimental literature of factors affecting unaided human
judgment. These apparent biases and shortcomings
will not be easily removed from organisational
decision making. The extent to which decision aids
can assist has not been evaluated; they seem to offer
the most immediately applicable partial solution
however. Since we have the cognitive capacity to
mediate in situations of decisional conflict it makes
sense to use whichever aids to decision making can
be shown to facilitate rational analysis. Any
decision aid capable of facilitating the conditions
required for what Janis and Mann (1977) have referred
to as vigilant decision making would be of value to
individuals and organisations.

Heuristics in Decision Making

Thorngate (1980) used a computer simulation
model to study hypothetical human decision heuristics.
His results, although theoretical, indicated that a

wide variety of decision heuristics will produce
optimal or close to optimal outcomes. Many of the
heuristics he modelled used only a small fraction
of the total available information. He concluded
that use of decision heuristics by humans is
determined by motivational factors as much as
cognitive limitations.

Tversky (1972) has pointed out the tendency
among people to be reluctant to accept the necessity
for subjective estimates in their decision making.
Instead, they seek an analysis of the situation
capable of incorporating a compelling principle of
choice which will resolve the decision without relying
on estimation of relative factor weights. He concluded
that people have more confidence in the rationality of
their decisions than they have in their own estimates.
Since decisions are made inevitably on subjective
judgments, it follows that any technique that improves
the reliability of estimates will be useful. The
processes of bolstering decisions outlined by Janis
and Mann (1977) would go some way to explain Tversky's
observations, since they serve to minimise anticipatory
and post decisional regret.

Fundamental to the success of any strategy for
improving the effectiveness of decision making in
organisations is the ability to improve the capacity
of the individual to analyse decision problems in a

way that minimises the risk of information overload. If this can be achieved, the individual is able to feel less frustrated in his efforts to deal with uncertainty and complexity. Without clearly defined goals the individual experiences varying degrees of frustration. Sommerhoff (1972) argues that the function of the brain is the selection of goals and the organisation of goal seeking behaviour. Goal directedness is claimed by Sommerhoff to be an objective system property which can be expressed mathematically. Not all goal directed behaviour is conscious: much of the life sustaining behaviour is claimed to be embodied in the older brain. It is the conscious striving after some future goal which is retained as some image structure which can be visualised, partially or completely, in the active imagination of the human organism. It seems probable that a hierarchy of decision heuristics exists.

This hierarchy of heuristics is conjectured to diversify in parallel with the individuals' development. It has been demonstrated that children are able to use cognitively more complex problem solving strategies as they develop. Cognitive development is probably not alone in determining the formation of decision heuristics in the mature adult. Moral development, particularly salient experiences of success and failure, and modelling based on the behaviour of members of reference groups are likely to contribute substantially to their development.

This interlocking system of decision rules is required to deal with both strategic planning and tactical decision making. In the former, the organism's foresight and planning horizons are critical. It seems improbable that such a faculty could be developed significantly in the mature adult: there simply is no evidence one way or the other, based on empirical study. For such skill to be enhanced, it would require ongoing training for some time; beginning in adolescence and continuing into adulthood. This view is based on the evidence for the development of abstract concept formation taking place at an accelerating pace in adolescence (Ginsberg & Opper, 1979, Chap. 5).

If such an hierarchy of decision heuristics develops in the human organism, it seems likely that each individual has unique cognitive biases. In certain circumstances there will be a greater tendency to under- or over-generalise than in others. It has been demonstrated that it is insufficient to point these out. (Tversky & Kahneman (1974), Bar Hillel (1974), Lyon & Slovic (1976)).

Such cognitive biases may well have been over-stated on the basis of the research evidence available. Slovic, Fischhoff & Lichtenstein (1977) pose the question: can normative experts be created from

substantive experts? The evidence for the effectiveness of training is mixed. Critics of decision
aids that rely on decomposition of the task, argue
that the aids require psychologically more complex
operations than the original decision. Slovic,
Fischhoff & Lichtenstein (1977) cite several earlier
studies in which the authors concluded that judgment
was aided by decomposing the task.

Lichtenstein and Fischhoff (1980) reviewed
recent research findings on the effect of training
on the subjective probability assessments of decision
makers. They concluded that people are typically
overconfident; believing they know more than they
actually know. They reported that attempts to
improve proability assessments with laboratory training, had generally poor results. In their own study,
subjects received intensive instructions and feedback
on their performance on easy and difficult tasks over
two hundred trials. They found that training in
probability assessment worked best when the subjects
received personal and definitive feedback on their
performance. they also found that one third of their
subjects, all of whom were highly educated, were well
calibrated in probability assessment before the
training. This group did not improve their performance following training. Among the remaining two
thirds, training failed to generalise to several
apparently related tasks.

Implications of Social Science Research for Training in Decision Aiding

Lichtenstein & Fischhoff's (1980) study had important implications for training in decision aiding. If training on such specific tasks fails to produce generalised effects on similar tasks, it appears unlikely that training in decision aiding, using case study material will generalise to the complexity of real life decisions. Thus, training is less likely to generalise to circumstances in which the decision maker is experiencing uncertainty. Stokes and Baer (1977) point out that generalisation has been viewed by psychologists as a naturally occurring, passive phenomenon. They emphasize "how very small the current technology is and how much development it requires." p 364.

Baddeley (1981) refers to what he terms the "Dustbowl empiricist" approach to the problems of cognitive psychology. He acknowledges that The plea for what Brunswik would term 'ecological validity' is not a new one . In studying the cognitive psychology of every day life he suggests the necessity of relating theory to problems outside the laboratory.

Morris (1981) argued in support of Ericson and Simon (1980) that strategy statements are useful in helping our understanding of cognitive processes.

He distinguished between strategy statements and
self hypotheses. Subjects, he argued, are able to
give reliable reports of their consciously chosen
strategies for tackling problems. He conceded the
point made by Nisbett and Wilson (1977), that they
may not be able to accurately describe the causal
processes that brought the behaviour about. This,
he argued, is no reason for rejecting strategy statements.

> Without the use of strategy statements I
> do not see how we can hope to understand
> cognitive processes of people in the sort
> of situations which the real world presents.
> p 468.

In this study it was assumed that people can
give at least reasonably accurate statements of the
strategies they typically adopt when faced with
decision problems. It cannot be demonstrated a
priori that this is a reasonable assumption, however
the author believes it to be supported by the weight
of existing evidence. Behling (1980) pleaded the
case for the natural science model for research in
organisational behaviour and organisation theory.
He would undoubtedly agree that cognitive and affective
processes of problem solving and decision making cannot be directly observed. He estimated that it would
be the weight of evidence and not crucial studies that

develop our understanding of the laws governing behaviour in organisations.

Decision making and problem solving are the main constituents of task behaviour in organisations. The processes by which such important behaviour is shaped and modified in organisational settings demand an eclectic approach to inquiry by researchers in the field. The present study of the effects of training in decision aiding procedures attempted to integrate some of the rigour of the natural science paridigm with an holistic approach. The research questions were impossible to define precisely in operational terms. To have done so would have required the sacrifice of more ecological validity than the author was prepared to accept.

As organisational behaviour becomes increasingly specialised for the individual, the need for self management procedures also increases. Mahoney and Arnkoff (1979) cited in Manz and Sims (1980) suggested that goal attainment seems to possess strong reinforcing properties. According to Bandura (1977) the importance of modelling in organisational contexts has been underestimated. Manz and Sims have argued that an integration of cognitive and social learning theory provides a more powerful explanation of human behaviour in organisations than either theory alone.

Emery and Trist (1965) point out that traditional organisational structures are not capable of responding in a functional manner in conditions of turbulence in the environment. At times when the causal texture of the environment becomes increasingly uncertain, the consequences of action tend to become unpredictable. This unpredictability makes planning and decision making within the context of hierarchical organisations impractical. The organisation structure, far from providing order, as an aid to efficient attainment of goals, has become an impediment.

Management training has become institution-alized in many large organisations. It has developed in response to perceived needs to improve the skill of its members in a variety of activities. Problem solving and decision making has traditionally been taught by a variety of methods, most of these rely on the case study approach. The expectation on the part of the organisation has been that familiarity with techniques for analysing such case studies will transfer to decision making in the organisational milieu. Psychological theories of learning reviewed here suggest that this approach is unlikely to be effective. It has been increasingly the experience of the author that this is the case, particularly when the training relates to the complex cognitive behaviour involved in problem solving and decision making.

Burgoyne and Stuart (1978) have criticised traditional training methods. Specifically, they claim that "Lecture-type methods may induce passivity in the learner". p 55. The case method fares no better in their view;

> The case method, as well as bringing about
> learning grounded in concrete examples, may
> also "teach" the learner to treat his life
> like a series of case studies, in a cool,
> detached and dispassionate manner. p 55.

They are more optimistic concerning Action Learning methods, which focus on encouraging managers to learn in the process of working on real organisational problems. (Revans 1971), cited in Burgoyne & Stuart (1978)).

Argyris (1980) has suggested that the training faculty reinforce dependency in the trainees by displaying their own competence, without giving the trainees sufficient opportunity to demonstrate the learning they have acquired. He also suggested that the trainees themselves contributed to the low transferability of the ideas that they had learned. This second point was not elucidated by Argyris. It is deserving of great attention however since it could explain much of the variance between trainees in post training behaviour.

Evaluation of Training Programs

Easterby-Smith (1981) has reviewed the changing approaches to evaluating education and training programs. Each approach has some strengths and at least one weakness. He concludes:

It (training evaluation) is a murky
business. Most evaluations are a matter
of producing information that is as useful
as possible with resources and facilities
that always seem to be inadequate. The
implementation of an evaluation study
never conforms to its blueprint. The skill
of the evaluator is exercised in collecting
the minimal amount of information required
to provide a fair picture.   p 36.

Cook and Campbell (1976) discuss the myth of "Hawthorn Effects" in field studies and conclude that the evidence is very weak. Although the conditions under which "hypothesis guessing" are not clearly understood, Bradburn, Sudman and Associates (1979) found that self administered procedures were slightly better than other methods for reducing overstatements.

The present study attempted to minimise response bias by adopting data collection procedures that were both non-threatening and as open ended as possible. Bradburn, Sudman & Associates (1979) found that interviewers only account for seven percent of response variance. It was decided therefore, that in order to maximise the validity of data to be used in the analysis, a combination of self administered questionnaire and loosely structured interview methods would be appropriate. Light (1979) concluded that any study of behaviour in organisations requires an holistic approach. He argued that any study of programs of training that only measure surface behaviour is at best incomplete. The lesson we have learned from Gallup and Harris he points out, is that if one asks a question, an answer will be forthcoming; albeit a stupid and meaningless one. Holistic analysis is important in this context because it examines the structural forces that shaped the individual in the first place. Van Maanen (1979) comments on the supposed match to be sought between research problem and method. In studies where the conceptual variables have not been capable of operational definition, he recommends the flexible integration of quantitative and qualitative techniques of analysis.

Morgan (1980) in a radical philosophical analysis of organisation theories, claims that theories of normative economic rationality owe their acceptance to the functionalist paradigm. This paradigm is based on the assumption that social organisation has a real and concrete existence whose purpose is the continuation of an ordered and

regulated state of affairs. For Morgan, any
normative theory of decision making would amount to
what Whitehead (1925), cited in Morgan (1980),
described as a 'useful fiction' for dealing with the
world. As such it would not be concerned with how
humans can link thought and action in the interests
of their own development.

Psychologists interested in aids to human
judgment have an inescapable responsibility to
maintain a vigilant outlook on the human implications
of such developments.

Research Questions

The principal aim of this study was to
evaluate the effects of training in a decision aiding
procedure. The two organisations in which the training
was carried out differed considerably in their
organisational structure and purpose. It could be
said that in Shell, the training has been in Phillips'
(1980) terms, institutionalised. Australia Post has
an active training function but has not previously
undertaken training of this type. In the case of
this organisation, the training was designed to meet
an identified need among a group of professionals and
managers in the headquarters. The need had originally
been identified as arising from the poor preparation
and presentation of recommendations to senior management. These recommendations formed the basis for

managements' policy submissions to The Australian
Postal Commission. They originated from several key
departments within the headquarters of Australia Post.
These departments were required to produce balanced
recommendations for policy changes. Data from these
recommendations originated from departments outside
the headquarters. In many cases this information
was not readily available and had to be actively
sought by the departments concerned. The objective
of the pilot training program was to systematically
improve this data collection and assembly into
alternative recommendations for final consideration
by senior management.

Several general research questions were
investigated, as were seven specific research
questions relating to the outcomes of the training.

The general research questions were:

AUSTRALIA POST

    (1) Had the training carried out in
           November/December 1980 resulted
           in improvements in ability to
           formulate and present decision
           options. If so, to what extent.
           If not, why not.

(2) To identify current attitudes and beliefs among those who had received the training, concerning their decision making and problem solving ability. Further: to compare these attitudes and beliefs, to those currently held by a matched group of untrained personnel.

(3) To identify other psychological variables affecting problem solving and decision making in the headquarters of Australia Post.

SHELL AUSTRALIA

(1) To what extent was the ongoing training in problem solving and decision making resulting in improved ability to perform these activities, as perceived by those who had received training and those who had not yet received it.

(2) As in (3) Australia Post.

BOTH ORGANISATIONS

(1) To examine relationships between information processing style as measured by The Information Processing Style Inventory, and:

(a) outcomes of the training program in decision making and problem solving.

(b)   The perceived difficulty of several
areas of problem solving, decision
making and planning. This was
measured by asking each subject to
rank five types of activity in order
of difficulty for them personally.
The activities in question appear
in Appendix 2.

(2)   To examine organisational variables affecting
the perceived value of the training. (i.e.
to compare an hierarchically organised headquarters staff group in a Government instru-
mentality, with a large commercial organisation.)

Specific Research Questions

(1)   It was conjectured that a Principal
Components Analysis of subjects' responses
to the Decision Making Questionnaire would
reveal several independent factors. It was
further conjectured that subjects' factor
scores on some or all of these factors would
discriminate between trained and untrained
subjects.

(2)   It was conjectured that a discriminant
analysis of factor scores would result in
a significant classification of subjects
into groups: further, that these groups
would be separately composed of trained
subjects and untrained subjects.

(3)   It was conjectured that if the training
      had resulted in changes in habitual decision
      making behaviour, differences in information
      processing styles would be identified
      between trained and untrained subjects.

(4)   It was conjectured that if the training
      had resulted in changes in habitual decision
      making behaviour, differences in the rank
      ordering of activities related to decision
      making, problem solving and organisation
      of planning would be apparent between trained
      and untrained groups.

(5)   It was expected that an hierarchical cluster
      analysis of subjects would reveal inter-
      pretable groupings of subjects.

(6)   It was expected that the data collected from
      the interviews with each subject would throw
      light on what was considered to be most
      useful about the training and what was least
      useful.

(7)   It was expected that any effects attributable
      to training would be more apparent among the
      Shell Australia Group. The reason being that
      Shell have had an ongoing organisational
      commitment to such training.

Method

Design & Materials

The main study reported here was preceded by a pilot study. The purpose of this pilot study was to facilitate the composition of data collection instruments, capable of measuring the most relevant variables in decision behaviour in organisations.

Eight persons participated in the pilot study including the author, who has had experience of training managers in decision aiding procedures in several large organisations.

The remaining seven members of the pilot study team were managers from commercial organisations. Three of these managers had experienced the training in their own organisations and the remaining four were experienced managers without formal training in decision aiding procedures.

Three data collection instruments were developed by the author, and tested on the pilot group for clarity and relevance.

The first of these instruments, the Decision Making Questionnaire, was designed for completion by subjects in conditions which protected their anonymity. Each item on the 57 item questionnaire had five alternative responses. 70% of the questionnaire items had been previously tested for reliability on a sample of 80 undergraduates of Melbourne University

(Morris, Note 1). Table 1 depicts summary statistics and reliability coefficients of the Decision Making Questionnaire. (A copy of the Decision Making Questionnaire & instructions appears in Appendix B, together with detailed reliability data and ANOVA statistics).

Table 1

Summary Statistics and Reliability Coefficients of Decision Making Questionnaire

n = 54

	Mean Score			S.D.
Scale	203			33
	Mean	Min	Max	Range
Item Means	3.56	1.94	4.54	2.6
Corrected Item (Total Correlations ranged from:	.28	to	.81	
Cronback Alpha for the Scale	.97			
Standardized item Alpha	.97			

The second research instrument, the Information Processing Style Inventory consisted of 15 pairs of questions. The 15 pairs were made up of six questions uniquely paired with each other. The six questions were

(1) Is it more likely that you would overlook possible adverse consequences when making decisions? or:

(2) Change your mind after making an important decision? or:

(3) Experience feelings of conflict leading to inertia and anxiety concerning change? or:

(4) Attempt to take too much information into
     account in making a decision and get over-
     loaded? or:

(5) Put off an unpleasant decision? or:

(6) Jump to conclusions prematurely in your
     decision making? or:

The inventory was presented verbally to each subject
by the author following a brief explanation of its
experimental nature. Each subject was advised that
the resulting profile of his style would be discussed
with him to check its validity. Without exception,
subjects felt the resulting scores on each question
accurately reflected their style of operating.
Many reported the exercise as having given them some
useful insights into their approach to problem solving and decision making.

        In addition to the authors previously mentioned,
upon whose work the Information Processing Style
Inventory was based, the author acknowledges the
contribution made to his thoughts on information
overload, by Miller (1960) cited in Katz & Kahn (1978).

        In summary, then, the I.P.S.P. had six
elements.

     Element 1. Propensity to overlook adverse
          consequences of preferred decision alternatives.

     Element 2. Post decisional regret: evidenced by
          propensity to change even quite important
          decisions after initial commitment.

Element 3. Anticipatory regret: evidenced by
propensity to conflict and anxiety when
facing decisions requiring change.

Element 4. Information overload: as evidenced
by propensity to attempt the processing of
more information than capacity allows in
time available for decision.

Element 5. Consideration of a narrow range of
options: as evidenced by the tendency to
jump to conclusions prematurely.

Element 6. Defensive avoidance: as evidenced
by the tendency to put off unpleasant
decisions.

The I.P.S.I. had the advantages of being quickly
administered, providing material for discussion in
the following interview and generating some useful
feedback to subjects.

The format of the instrument resulted in
distribution of 15 responses across six elements,
each of which could have a range of scores from
0 to 5. Scores on each element were approximately
normally distributed in the sample. (The Information
Processing Style Inventory appears in Appendix B).

The instrument was considered to be useful
in exploring relationships between the effects of
training in decision procedures and individual
differences in information processing style.

The third data collection instrument was

included in order to identify differences between trained and untrained subjects in perceived difficulty of handling the commonly confronted cognitive activities involved in organisations. Each of these can be difficult, depending on circumstances. It was expected that any significant differences revealed between matched groups of subjects, engaged in similar jobs, could be related, at least in part, to the effects of training. In this way it was hoped to identify any differential effects of the training program.

The following activities were considered:

(1) Long range planning.

(2) Planning your routine, week to week activities, in order to achieve short term objectives.

(3) Keeping track of all the relevant information you need to make short range decisions.

(4) Analyzing complex interrelated problems.

(5) Coming up with novel and workable solutions to work problems.

Subjects were requested to rank these activities from most to least difficult. Recognising that such a procedure is dependent not only on job characteristics but on demands of the moment, subjects were asked to rank the activities in the general context of their present position. The Cognitive

Activities Inventory appears in Appendix B.

Design of Interviews

Each subject was interviewed at his or her
normal place of work by the author. Interviews were
considered a necessary component of the data collection procedure for the following reasons:

(1)   Interviews give the subject an opportunity
to tell the researchers what he or she believes
relevant to the research question. In this case,
organisational variables were of interest, particularly
as they affected training in decision procedures.
The interviews provided a rich source of data.
Without them, this research would have been much
diminished.

To provide a focus for each interview,
and as a means of standardizing the context of the
data collection, the early part of the interview was
structured systematically. As a preliminary step,
each subject was presented with a simple schematic
model of the decision process. This was described
briefly and related to decision making in organizational contexts. (The model appears in Appendix B).

As interviews were carried out during normal
working yours, each was expected to be limited to 40 minutes duration. In this time, eight questions relating to

the difficulties experienced with decision making
processes were discussed. As the interviews
progressed, subjects were able to expand their own
views. As expected, there appear to be several
unintended consequences of training in decision
aiding procedures. These would not have been
revealed to this researcher had he used only pencil
and paper methods of data collection. Indeed, the
results using only these methods, would have been
not only incomplete, but potentially misleading.
(The eight questions forming the structured part
of the interview, together with a sample response
appear in Appendix B).

Selection of Organisations for Study

Australia Post was approached by the author
to participate in this study. As the trainer involved,
the author wished to assess the effects of his work
in that organisation. The Training Department agreed
to cooperate in order to gain a better understanding
of the outcomes of such training. It was with their
much appreciated assistance, that a control group of
untrained subjects was identified.

Shell Australia was approached to participate
in the study for four reasons:

(1) That organisation had a commitment to the
decision training procedures recommended by Kepner &
Tregoe (1965). The Company has been training managers

and professional staff in the procedures for problem
solving and decision making recommended by Kepner &
Tregoe (1965) for ten years. It was possible for
them to identify subjects who had not been through
the training program however, since individual
participation was determined by several factors.
Among these, seniority, length of service, job
requirements and the need for development of analytical skills were important. The control group
identified in that organisation were "eligible" to
participate; they had not done so, but it was
expected that they would in the course of time.

(2) The organisational objectives of Shell
Australia differ from those of Australia Post.
Shell is operating in an oligopolist market.
Australia Post is nominally a monopoly, although
this is changing as free enterprise continues to
carry an increasing share of the small parcel market.
It was conjectured that Phillips' (1980) assertions
could best be explored by choosing an organisation
in which decision aiding in some form, had been
"institutionalised".

(3) The organisation structure in Shell differs
from that in Australia Post. It is hierarchical in
the same way that most organisations are. The shape
is different however. Australia Post is characterised
by a very steep hierarchy, Shell by a relatively flat

structure with less formalized boundaries. The patterns of communication, and the informal organisation structure differ widely between the two organisations. Although both organisations are large, in other respects they are quite dissimilar. If the socio-technical structure has a significant influence on the way in which training in decision aiding is integrated into a system, it was expected that it would be observed in this study.

(4) Shell Australia have a reputation for maintaining very high standards of training among their training professionals. The training program offered to their staff in analytical skills and decision procedures reflects these high standards. Although no two trainers and no two training programs are identical, it was expected that a fair comparison was possible between the two organisations in terms of the content and quality of the training.

Both groups were selected by a member of the Training Department at Shell. Names of trained personnel were selected randomly. These persons were then matched with eligible but untrained members of Shell.

It has been mentioned that no two training programs are identical. In the case of the decision aiding training under study here, it is suggested that the differences are peripheral, being differences of emphasis rather than substance. (A detailed description of the training program content appears in Appendix B).

Shell Australia were in the process of carry-ing out a training needs analysis at the time this study commenced. The author agreed to share the research findings with the Company. The same agree-ment was made with Australia Post. (This agreement was made subject to the approval of Prof. Wearing). In the trade off between experimental control and ecological validity, the latter has been purchased at some expense to the former. In this quasi-experimental study of decision aiding training, error was kept as low as possible by careful attention to sample selection and matching of control groups.

Attempts to understand naturally occurring purposeful behaviour demand the infringement of some ideals of experimental method. In order to understand the processes of human decision making, it is necessary to consider the environment in which these processes take place. In the present study, no pre-treatment measures were possible, it was expected that such measures would be suggested in the process of this inquiry.

Subjects

54 subjects participated in the study. 38 were managers or senior professionals in the head-quarters of Australia Post. 16 were managers or senior professionals in Shell Australia.

It was originally planned that 20 trained subjects from Australia Post would participate. Owing to sickness, one participant had to withdraw. There were therefore 19 trained subjects, and a matched group of 19 untrained subjects.

The trained subjects had been selected from four departments in Australia Post to participate in a training program in decision making and problem solving. This program was completed in December 1980.

16 subjects from the Shell Australia Company participated. 20 had been planned, but pressure of work forced the withdrawal of two of the trained subjects. The remaining 8 trained subjects and their matched control group participated.

The most recently trained subject had received the training in 1981. The remaining subjects had received their training between 1972 and 1980.

All participants from both organisations were aware that the study comprised one part of the final assessment for an honours degree in psychology at Melbourne University. They received no pecuniary reward for their participation. Without exception they showed willing and cooperative participation.

Both groups of subjects were employed in the headquarters of the organisation for whom they worked. Each of these headquarters is located in central Melbourne.

Each subject was informed that the strictest confidence would be maintained concerning his or her data. It was also explained that an aggregation of data would be made available to each organisation if they wished to examine the results.

Table 2 provides a summary of the demographic data used in the analysis of results.

Table 2

		Trained Group	Control Group
Total Number of Subjects 54		27	27
Sex:	Males	24	24
	Females	3	3
Age:	Mean	39.8	41.0
	Median	38.7	42.2
	S.D.	8.4	12.1
Length of Service	Mean	10.2	11.7
	Median	7.9	9.7
	S.D.	8.2	9.1
Number of Subordinates in Organisa- tion	Mean	5.8	2.9
	Median	0.47	2.0
	S.D.	15.3	3.3

Education Level

2 = Leaving Certificate

3 = Matriculation

4 = Diploma/Technical

5 = University Degree

6 = Postgraduate

	Mean	3.9	4.1
	Median	3.8	4.1
	S.D.	.85	1.56

Cont/.

Table 2 - continued

	Trained Group	Control Group
Level in Organisation		
1 = Admin/Professional		
2 = Supervisor		
3 = Manager		
Mean	1.7	1.7
Median	1.5	1.7
M.D.	.78	.81

Procedure

Briefing Meetings:

As a preliminary step in this study, subjects in Australia Post attended a briefing meeting. At this meeting the author outlined the purpose of the research program and thanked the subjects for their willingness to participate. Two meetings were held on consecutive mornings in order to ensure that as many subjects as possible would be able to attend.

Subjects were advised that they would each receive a Decision Making Questionnaire, to be sent to them in the internal mail system. They were asked to complete the questionnaire according to the instructions enclosed with it. Subjects were advised that the author would contact them individually to arrange a mutually convenient time for a brief meeting, expected to last for between 30 and 45 minutes.

Subjects were requested not to discuss the questionnaire with other participants, at least until all interviews had been completed. This was expected to take two weeks in all.

Briefing meetings were not practicable in Shell owing to pressure of workload in that organisation. Each participant was contacted by telephone however and briefed by the author.

Questionnaire Administration

The Decision Making Questionnaires were distributed through the internal mail system in each organisation. Each was sent in a sealed envelope. Enclosed with each questionnaire was a stamped addressed envelope for its return to the author. One questionnaire was lost in the post; the subject concerned completed a duplicate.

Fully completed questionnaires were received from all subjects participating in the study.

Each questionnaire was coded to protect the anonymity of respondents and permit identification by the author for purposes of data analysis.

Interview Conditions

A private interview was conducted with each subject. Appointments were made to suit subjects, and the interviews took place either in the subjects' office or some suitably quiet room if no private office was available. Interviews ranged in duration from 30 to 60 minutes.

Each interview was opened by the author giving a one or two minute presentation of the simple model of decision making and its relevance to decision processes in the work environment.

Following this presentation, subjects were asked to consider the five types of cognitive activity in relation to their present job. Each subject was then asked to rank them in descending order of difficulty. Subjects were encouraged to take a few minutes to think about this task before deciding on a rank order.

When this had been completed, the Information Processing Style Inventory was introduced. Subjects were advised that they were going to be presented with 15 pairs of statements, each of which described a commonly experienced difficulty in decision making. It was pointed out to subjects that this was an experimental task, and that they should choose the statement which, on the balance of probabilities, best described their own experience. It was pointed out that no pair of statements would be repeated, although each separate statement, would appear several times in combination with others. Subjects were invited to ask the researcher to repeat the statements whenever they wished. No reference was made to the title of the inventory. Subjects were advised they could "pass" any pair of statements if they wished.

When all 15 pairs of statements had been presented, element scores were totalled and discussed with the subject. Subjects were asked to comment on the validity of their set of element scores.

On completion of the I.P.S.I., normally 15-20 minutes after the start of the interview, each subject was asked the same sequence of eight questions concerning decision making in their organisation. Answers were summarized and written in note form by the author. Paraphrasing was used to check clear understanding of answers.

Interviews were completed over a two week period. Subjects in Australia Post were interviewed on seven consecutive working days. Subjects in Shell were interviewed during the remaining three days of the second week. Trained subjects were interviewed before untrained subjects in each organisation.

Following data collection, 80 column coding forms were used for data preparation. Two records per subject were required. Cards were keypunched and verified by Adaps Computer Services of Melbourne.

Data was analysed using the Control Data Corporation Cyber installation in the Computer Centre, University of Melbourne. In addition to the use of SPSS programs, the university Veldman Program was used for Hierarchical Cluster Analysis.

Results and Discussion

Format

In the interests of brevity, this section commences with results relating to each of the specific research questions. A brief discussion follows each result. The general discussion follows these specific findings and draws together the results obtained from the research instruments and the interviews.

Principal Components Analysis of the Decision Making Questionnaire

Summary descriptive statistics for the total item content of the Decision Making Questionnaire have been reported in Table 1 on page 68 of the Design and Materials Section.

A principal components analysis of the scores on all items from each of the 54 subjects was performed in order to identify subscales. Items were included in the subscales only if the largest percentage of variance relating to the item was accounted for in the relevant factor. The factor solution was derived from a varimax rotation without iteration.

13 factors were derived with eigenvalues greater than 1. The analysis was based on the first 6 factors however, since the lowest of these accounted for only 3.4% of total variance.

The percentage of total variance accounted for by each of the 6 factors appears in Table 3.

Table 3

Percentage of Total Variance explained by each of the First 6 Factors Derived from the Principal Components Analysis of the Decision Making Questionnaire

Factors	% of Total Variance
Factor 1	39.2
Factor 2	6.1
Factor 3	4.6
Factor 4	4.2
Factor 5	3.6
Factor 6	3.4
% of Total Variance	61.1

A complete summary of the rotated factor solution, including eigenvalues and factor matrix appears in Appendix C.

Each of the subscales constructed from the principal components analysis was labelled according to the dimension of decision related behaviour it best described. 41 of the total of 57 items in the questionnaire appeared in the subscales. Each item in any subscale was permitted to contribute equally in the calculation of factor scores for subjects.

This approximation to true factor scores was considered to be adequate for an exploratory study of this nature.

Factor labels and the items comprising each subscale are described in Table 4.

Table 4

Factor Labels and Items Loading Principally

on each Factor Respectively

Factor Number and Label	Items
Factor 1 - "Confidence in Decision Making Judgments"	6, 9, 16, 23, 28, 30, 31, 38, 39, 42, 46, 52, 54
Factor 2 - "Collection and Organisation of Decision Making Information"	10, 25, 29, 32, 35, 37, 44, 55
Factor 3 - "Calm, Patient Approach"	15, 26, 47, 48
Factor 4 - "Active Independence"	2, 3, 23, 34, 35, 40, 51, 53
Factor 5 - "Control over Outcomes"	11, 14, 20, 50
Factor 6 - "Overconfidence"	17, 30, 42

The group means and S.D.'s for each factor are reported in Table 5.

Table 5

Group Means and S.D.'s of Factor Scores for
each Group of Trained and Untrained Subjects

Group		Factor 1	Factor 2	Factor 3	Factor 4	Factor 5	Factor 6
Australia Post:[a]							
Trained:	Mean	46.4	30.7	13.8	31.4	19.0	9.9
	S.D.	7.7	3.6	3.2	5.1	2.1	1.9
Untrained:	Mean	44.8	29.5	13.1	32.5	18.1	9.2
	S.D.	6.4	4.4	2.1	4.5	3.6	2.0
Shell [b]							
Trained:	mean	47.9	31.5	14.1	33.4	19.3	10.0
	S.D.	4.5	1.8	1.1	3.5	1.8	1.8
Untrained:	Mean	45.8	29.8	14.5	32.6	18.9	9.4
	S.D.	8.0	3.5	1.1	3.0	2.2	1.2

[a] n = 19 for each group

[b] n = 8 for each group.

Discriminant Analysis of Factor Scores & 't' Tests

The factor scores obtained for each subject
on each of the 6 factors described, formed the data for
a discriminant analysis. This multivariate one way
analysis of variance was performed on the data from
the four groups in the study.

The result of the discriminant analysis
showed no significant difference between groups on any
factor. (A summary of this analysis appears in
Appendix C).

Subjects were classified into groups as part of the discriminant analysis program. This classification showed that neither trained Australia Post subjects nor those trained in Shell were correctly classified at levels better than chance. 58% of those trained in Australia Post were correctly classified; 38% of those trained in Shell were classified correctly.

This result was in the reverse direction to that expected. The assertion made by Phillips (1980), that the benefits of decision aiding technology are only fully realised when they have been institution- alised in an organisation is not supported by this result. His assertion has a degree of validity however, as later results to be discussed here, will demonstrate.

Mean scores of trained subjects were higher than untrained subjects on 52 items and equal on two items. (Mean scores on each item for the trained and untrained groups are included in Appendix C).

Only one item was found to have a statistically significant difference however. A two tailed t test revealed a significant difference in mean scores on item 53, t (52) = -2.83, p = .007. Trained subjects were therefore indicating by their higher average score on that item, that they are less likely to reject an otherwise good alternative that is in conflict with the wishes of important others.

The most reasonable explanation of this finding is perhaps that trained subjects have been provided with a more systematic method of probing the reasons and objectives underlying other people's decisions. Such a systematic exploration may result in a willingness to negotiate a position, or alternatively an increased tendency towards non compliance in general. The result is consistent with other data obtained in the course of interviews. In this respect this significant result will be referred to again later in the discussion.

Hierarchical Cluster Analysis of Subjects, using all items from the Decision Making Questionnaire

Several hierarchical cluster analyses of subjects were performed using all 57 items from the Decision Making Questionnaire. By this method it was hoped to identify individuals and groups of subjects with similar score profiles, using more of the available data than was used in the principal components analysis. Analyses were completed on groups assembled by organisation, by total score on the questionnaire, (a high score and low score group), by age, by sex and by seniority. In no instance did the resulting classifications of trained subjects yield significant values on

Chi square tests. No detectable patterns of scores on the Questionnaire were found, related to any of the other objective characteristics of the sample.

The percentage of correctly classified subjects from the Australia Post sample, in the discriminant analysis, which used only 61% of total variance, was greater than any of the analyses performed using hierarchical cluster analysis.

The analysis of subjects by age in Shell, correctly classified 71% of those aged over the median age. The result, although not significant statistically, is of interest as it may be relevant to a later result.

No group in the hierarchical cluster analysis of all Shell subjects contained more than 62% of the trained subjects. This was approximately as expected by chance. (A Summary of hierarchical Cluster data appears in Appendix C).

Information Processing Style Inventory Results

Descriptive statistics relating to each element of the I.P.S.I. are reported in Table 6.

Table 6

Means, S.D.'s and Distribution Characteristics

of Information Processing Style Elements.

Trained and Untrained Groups Respectively

Information Processing		Groups	
Style Elements		Trained[a]	Untrained[b]
Element 1: Propensity to overlook Adverse Consequences of Preferred Options	Mean S.D. Stewness	2.26 1.40 .13	1.41 .97 .15
Element 2: Post Decisional Regret: As Evidenced by Propen- sity to Change Even Quite Important Decisions After Commit- ment	Mean S.D. Stewness	2.78 1.19 -.43	2.93 1.52 -.58
Element 3: Anticipatory Regret: As evidenced by Propen- sity to Experience Conflict and Anxiety when Facing Decisions Requiring Change	Mean S.D. Stewness	3.26 1.32 -.41	2.85 1.1 -.62
Element 4: Information Overload: As Evidenced by Propen- sity to Attempt the Processing of More Information than Capacity Permits in Time Available for Decision	Mean S.D. Stewness	2.37 1.84 1.23	2.82 1.57 -.25
Element 5: Consideration of narrow range of Options: as Evidenced by the Tendency to Jump to Premature Conclusions	Mean S.D. Stewness	2.00 1.62 .41	2.52 1.50 118
Element 6: Defensive Avoidance: as Evidenced by the Tendency to Put off Unpleasant Decisions	Mean S.D. Stewness	2.33 1.41 .15	1.93 1.39 .24

[a] n = 27
[b] n = 27

A discriminant analysis of the first 5 information processing style elements revealed a statistically significant first discriminant function, discriminating between the trained and untrained group in Australia Post. Chi square test (5) = 17.16, $p<.005$.

The sixth element failed to pass the tolerance test of the Discriminant Program of SPSS. This element was examined separately using Chi Square tests. No significant differences were found between groups in either Australia Post or Shell on this element.

A discriminant analysis of the first five information processing style elements between the Shell trained and untrained groups did not yield a statistic-ally significant discriminant function. (Copies of the discriminant analysis are included in Appendix C).

Trained subjects in Australia Post scored significantly higher on the first element and signifi-cantly lower on the fifth element. Significantly higher scores on the first element were contrary to expectations as it was expected that a trained group would be less likely to overlook adverse consequences of decision alternatives than an untrained group.

The significantly lower scores on the fifth element was in line with the expectations that a trained group would be less likely to jump to conclusions pre-maturely.

A possible explanation for the observation that trained subjects in Australia Post score more highly on the first element is that the training has sensitized this group to the need for consideration of possible adverse consequences of decision options. Being sensitized to the desirability of such action, and being able to reliably foresee such consequences in practice are quite separate issues. It is quite feasible that trained subjects would appreciate the need to make more systematic attempts to foresee such consequences and yet report failing to do so. This seems to be particularly likely if their attempts had not fulfilled their expectations.

This result may also be explained in part by the nature of the work done by subjects in Australia Post. In the main, they are concerned with preparing written recommendations, presenting alternative policy options and evaluating the supporting arguments for each. Their performance appraisal and prospects of promotion in the organisation are dependent to a large extent on the quality of these recommendations as perceived by higher management.

The program of training in decision making and problem solving undertaken by subjects in Australia Post, was specifically aimed at assisting them with the preparation of well reasoned recommendations. It seems quite likely that the nature of the task, and the specific emphasis on these aspects in the training program, has resulted in the observed differences between trained and untrained in Australia Post.

The psychological implications for the individual who reports failing to take adverse consequences into account, when the importance of this step has been emphasized by an "expert in decision training" are potentially important. It could reasonably be expected that individuals would experience greater levels of frustration when attempting to formulate recommendations in an uncertain environment. The objective causal structure of the environment may not have changed significantly, but the trained subjects' perception of it, may have changed. If the decision maker perceives less certainty in the environment as a result of changes in his model of causal relationships, it is likely that this perception of uncertainty will manifest itself in some way in his cognitive behaviour. This conjecture is supported by the significantly higher level of dissatisfaction with goal clarity reported by the trained subjects in the interviews. This result is reported in detail in the interview results section.

Rank Ordering of Difficulty in Cognitive Activities

       The mean rank and S.D.'s of scores on the Cognitive Activities Inventory for subjects in Australia Post are reported in Table 7.

Table 7

Means and S.D.'s of the Rank Order of Difficulty in Cognitive Activities Inventory. Trained and Untrained Groups in Australia Post. (Low Scores indicate Greater Difficulty).

Cognitive Activities		Groups	
		Trained[a]	Untrained[b]
Long Range Planning	Mean	3.1	3.3
	S.D.	1.4	1.1
Planning your Routine week to week activities	Mean	3.2	4.0
	S.D.	1.5	1.1
Keeping Track of all the Relevant Information you need to make Short Range Decisions	Mean	3.1	3.1
	S.D.	1.5	1.6
Analysing Complex Interrelated Problems	Mean	3.2	2.5
	S.D.	1.5	1.4
Coming up with Novel and workable Solutions to work Problems	Mean	2.5	2.1
	S.D.	1.2	1.2

n^a = 19

n^b = 19

Table 8 depicts the same data for the Shell groups.

Table 8

Means & S.D.'s of the Rank Order of Difficulty in Cognitive Activities Inventory. Trained and Untrained Groups in Shell Australia. (Low Scores indicate Greater Difficulty).

Cognitive Activities		Groups	
		Trained[a]	Untrained[b]
Long Range Planning	Mean S.D.	2.8 1.2	2.8 1.2
Planning your Routine week to week activities	Mean S.D.	3.0 1.2	3.3 1.7
Keeping Track of all the relevant Information you need to make Short Range Decisions	Mean S.D.	3.3 1.8	3.4 1.4
Analysing Complex Interrelated Problems	Mean S.D.	2.6 1.3	3.4 1.4
Coming up with Novel and Workable Solutions to Work Problems	Mean S.D.	3.4 1.8	2.1 1.4

n^a = 8
n^b = 8

Discriminant analyses revealed no significant differences between groups on any of the cognitive activities included in the inventory.

It was conjectured that training in decision making procedures would influence perceptions of difficulty. It was also expected that any changes would be more observable among the Shell group. The latter conjecture has some surface validity when the data are inspected. Although the result is not statistically significant, the effect of training in analytical skills appears to be most marked in the Shell group. The largest mean rank difference is observed between the groups on the cognitive activity of developing novel and workable solutions to work problems.

Sex Differences: Information Processing Style

Significant differences were found between males and females on three of the six Information Processing Style elements. This result is presented despite its peripheral relevance to the research questions in this study, since an increasing number of women are joining the ranks of management and senior professional groups in large organisations. The assumptions made, largely by men, about what constitutes good management decision making in organisations, may require revision as an increasing number of professional women take their places at the boardroom table. Since the number of women in this study reflects their small representation in the population from which the sample was drawn, the statistic should be treated with caution.

Chi square tests revealed the following differences between the sexes. Males report less conflict when facing decisions requiring change: element 3 on I.P.S.I.

$X^2_{(1)}$ = 10.92, p<.001. Females report a smaller propensity to change their minds after making an important decision: element 2 on I.P.S.I. $X^2_{(1)}$ = 8.35, p<.01. Females report a greater propensity to put off unpleasant decisions: element 6 on I.P.S.I. $X^2_{(1)}$ = 5.78, p<.02.

It appears from these results that women are more likely to experience pre decisional conflict, but less likely to yield to the pressures for reversals of decisions once they are taken. Commitment for women may be interpreted as a more important part of the decision process. The implication of this finding, if it proved to be valid, could make for better balanced decision making teams in organisations that employed females and males in key decision roles.

This is an issue which has not been addressed in the literature on decision making. It is likely to become increasingly important in the future and is worthy of further investigation.

Interview Results

Question 1. What is your single biggest problem in decision making?

74% of the trained subjects in Australia Post gave lack of goal clarity as their single biggest problem. This compared to 37% of the untrained group. This result was statistically significant. Chi square $X_{(1)}$ = 5.22, p<.05.

The trained group in Australia Post were more concerned with situational than procedural uncertainty. Fear of commitment in the face of poor goal clarity was an issue, even for those whose statements did not identify poor goal clarity specifically as the single biggest problem.

In Shell there was no statistically significant single biggest problem. The cluster of problems described can best be classified as uncertainty arising from accelerating change. Lack of goal clarity was an important component as 5 of the 8 trained subjects reported that they felt goals were now less clearly defined than in previous times. The same proportion of untrained subjects mentioned lack of goal clarity as the single major difficulty. They did not state the view that goals were now less clearly defined than previously, however.

<u>Question 2. Tell me about the things that create most difficulty for you in problem solving and decision making?</u>

The objective of this question was to gain a broader perspective of the sorts of difficulties reported by trained and untrained subjects. The range of difficulties reported was wide. The most interpretable difference between the groups in Australia Post concerned fear of commitment expressed by 26% of the trained group. This was not a specifically expressed concern of the untrained group. The untrained group were more concerned with structuring problems. 37% reported having difficulty determining which decision making information was the most relevant. Both groups expressed concern with the lack of feedback they received from the organisation. One subject made the following comment, which encapsulated the level of uncertainty. "Often there are no compelling goals or 'right' solutions. It is difficult to test the expectations of the policy of this organisation by hypothesis. So when there are no possibilities for hypothesis testing, I fall back on basic heuristics and then on personal values."

In Shell the major difficulty was time pressure and the uncertainty created by rapid change. There were no detectable differences between trained and untrained subjects.

Question 3. What are the critical external variables affecting the way you make your decisions?

The major variable reported by both groups in Australia Post, was lack of decision making information attributed to overcentralization of decision making, and unwillingness to delegate responsibility. 74% of the trained group and 42% of the untrained group reported this view. This result was statistically significant. Chi square test

$\underline{X}^2_{(1)} = 3.89$, p<.05.

The trained group were generally more critical of what they perceived to be management's lack of confidence in their abilities as decision makers.

It is possible that this group were able to express their views more freely to the author on the basis of personal acquaintance.

Each group in Shell reported similar views. Economic uncertainty and market unpredictability were reported as contributing to uncertainty in the organisation. The resulting changes in priority and difficulty in formulating plans were considered to be the most critical external variables affecting decision making at the individual level.

Question 4. Do you find it useful to break decisions down into smaller components? If so, how do you do it?

68% of the trained subjects in Australia Post reported decomposition of decision tasks to be useful for discriminating between alternatives. They reported the process of decomposition to be most useful for aiding communication in groups of decision makers. The most important benefit was reported to be the way in which decision alternatives could be made publicly visible in a decision making group. Each of the members of the trained group appeared to have integrated parts of the decomposition procedure into his or her own set

of decision rules. Overall, the benefits were seen
as a communication aid and of only limited value as
an aid to judgment.

50% of the trained group in Shell were
sceptical of the value of decomposition as an aid in
decision making. 25% reported it useful as a "fail
safe" device, useful for preventing obvious oversights,
25% reported that the process of decomposition was
not compatible with their decision processes and they
therefore found it a hindrance. This 25% conceded
that other people in the organisation seemed to find
it useful, but principally as a communication aid.

Among members of the untrained groups,
decision rules were highly variable and personalised.
Most felt that a more systematic approach would be of
considerable value to them. In this context it is interesting to note that the responses to item 20 on the
Decision Making Questionnaire differed between the
trained and untrained in each organisation. Although
the differences were not statistically significant,
trained subjects in Shell gave a lower estimate of the
value of training in decision making. (2 tailed t test
(10) = -1.94 $p<.1$).

Trained subjects in Australia Post rated
training in decision making marginally higher than
untrained subjects. The difference was of no

statistical significance however (2 tailed $\underline{t}$ test (34)
= .77, $\underline{p}$<.5).

Question 5. If you were asked to explain your own
decision making process, how would you explain it?

Responses to this question were difficult to
categorise. There were no systematic differences
between trained and untrained subjects in either
organisation. Subjectively interpreted, the trained
subjects indicated greater efforts to systematically
organise decision related information. These subjects
mentioned the importance of defining clear objectives
before considering alternatives, more frequently than
untrained subjects. The sample response to this
question, quoted in Appendix B, is generally representative of the responses given by trained and untrained
subjects in both organisations.

Question 6. Could you tell me about your experiences
of uncertainty? When you feel uncertain, what seems
to cause it, what do you do to minimise uncertainty?

Subjects in Shell were markedly more concerned
with uncertainty than subjects in Australia Post. The
more senior managers in Australia Post expressed greater
concern with the problems of dealing with uncertainty
than the subjects with less responsibility for the work
of others.

Trained subjects in Shell were more concerned with situational uncertainty than the untrained group. The untrained group were concerned with procedural uncertainty, particularly related to information handling in problem solving and decision making. It appeared that the trained group were less concerned with setting priorities and more concerned with clarifying goals. Both groups considered that their performance in decision making could be significantly improved by greater effort on the part of senior management to pay more careful attention to the planning of change. Both groups in Shell considered that they were under additional time pressures resulting in inadequate analysis of decisions.

Question 7. What do you feel has contributed most to your ability as a problem solver and decision maker? Can you point to specific experiences and describe them?

100% of the subjects in Shell attributed their development to particularly stimulating periods in their lives. In each case this involved working for a person who gave them challenging work, feedback on their performance, and contributed significantly to their perceptions of their own self esteem and competence.

84% of the trained group in Australia Post reported similar experiences. 16% attributed their development to taking responsibility for themselves very early in life.

90% of the untrained group in Australia Post reported similar experiences to the majority in the other groups. One subject attributed his development to continuing education and one subject attributed his success as a decision maker to being out in the world, alone, from the age of 13.

In the overwhelming majority of cases, an important role model, sometimes more than one, but rarely more than two, were perceived as having shaped their lives and subsequent decision making ability. A brief synopsis of each subject's response to this question is included in Appendix B.

The author paid special attention to avoiding cues to subjects on this question, particularly after the first few interviews. Subjects were encouraged to say why they thought such experiences had occurred, and when. The responses indicated that these experiences are not confined to the young and inexperienced. The importance of significant role models appears to be pervasive well into middle age.

Question 8. How do you know when you are ready to make a decision that requires commitment?

The responses to this question indicated that the main sources of commitment were outside the conscious awareness of the individual. The affective structure of commitment to action is apparently a much stronger influence than the cognitive structure. Certainly the cognitive structure mediates, but it does not appear to have the last word. Many of the trained subjects made mention of the dissonance between their intellectual analysis of a decision and the conflict between this result and what they "really intended to do".

General Discussion

This study attempted to identify the variables affecting the usefulness to individuals of training in a simple decision aiding procedure. It was expected that significant differences would be found on at least some of the variables affecting decision makers faced with consequential choice.

In view of the consistently high ratings by persons having participated in such training in a variety of organisational settings, it was surprising to find no discernible differences in the factor scores derived from the Decision Making Questionnaire. Although Janis and Mann (1977) demonstrated the unreliability of hypothetical decision problems as a predictor of behaviour in real world settings, it was expected that such training would result in detectable changes in decision making strategy. The measures used in this study were experimental, and therefore untried as instruments of discrimination. It was considered that for their purpose they were adequate. If systematic training effects are being produced, resulting in behaviour changes in the domain of decision making, this study has failed to detect them.

It is suggested that individual decision makers each find some aspects of the training useful in different contexts. As a means of reducing the cognitive bias produced by what Tversky (1972) described as the "Representativeness Heuristic", the procedures recommended by Kepner and Tregoe (1965, 1981) appear to offer a potentially useful aid. This view is supported by the finding that trained subjects in Australia Post report a significantly lower tendency to jump to premature conclusions in their decision making.

The finding that the same group fail to take adverse consequences of decision alternatives into account is puzzling. It has been suggested earlier, that as a result of the training, these subjects are sensitive to the need to consider the threats to their decisions. It would appear that the training has not improved their ability to foresee such consequences. The psychological implications of this reported failure may result in increased conservatism in decision making.

Trained subjects in both organisations
reported the major strength of the decomposition procedure was its value as a communication aid in decision
making groups. In such settings, subjects reported
the procedures recommended by Kepner & Tregoe (1965,
1981) assisted in identification of the loci of dis-
agreements and the resolution of differences by
negotiation.

Training in procedural rationality appears to
have produced very little by way of systematic change in
the decision behaviour of individuals. Hogarth (1980)
asserted that techniques of task decomposition, while
not being a panacea for decision making, offered the
best available aid to decision makers. At the level of
the individual human decision maker, this assertion
appears unsupported by the evidence reported here.
Individual strategies for coping with perceived
complexity and uncertainty do not appear to be
influenced by procedural aids to decision making.

MacCrimmon and Taylor (1976) concluded that
the conceptual structure of the individual is the principal determinant of his ability to cope with complexity
and undertainty. The decision maker's ability to
structure problems into a manageable format depends on
his ability to manage his own perceptions of uncertainty.
The evidence from the present study suggests that
decision aids relying on what Hammond, McClelland and
Mumpower (1980) described as inductive knowing, do not

assist decision makers in dealing with their own perceptions of uncertainty and complexity.

The Importance of Goal Clarity in Decision Making

Humphreys and McFadden (1980) suggested that the efficacy of decision aids depended on the structuring of tasks to clarify goals. The results of this study indicate that in order to be useful to the decision maker, a decision aid should assist in clarifying his goals. The training appears to have increased the psychological salience of individual and organisational goals. It does not appear to have assisted decision makers with the task of structuring their goals however. In this respect, the training appears to have induced conditions of frustration in decision making activities. This frustration with lack of goal clarity was reported more frequently in Australia Post than in Shell. It was more frequently observed among the Shell trained subjects than the untrained however. The difference between the organisations in respect to this result has already been mentioned. It is considered less likely that subjects in Shell, having no previous knowledge of the author, would express psychological dissatisfaction with the capacity of their organisation to maintain satisfactory levels of goal clarity.

The evidence in support of training in

procedural rationality leading to greater frustration in decision related behaviour was supported by the significantly more critical attitudes toward senior management expressed by trained subjects. This more highly critical attitude was not related to particular actions or attributes of the more senior decision makers. It was manifest as frustration with the perceived impotence of senior management to set a clear goal structure for the organisation. Most of these subjects acknowledged that the more senior decision makers were also operating in conditions of greater environmental uncertainty.

At least for the two groups in this study, training in procedural rationality appears to have reduced individual tolerance for ambiguity in the organisation. This may be a constructive force for change if it results in the establishment of clearer goals. In relatively turbulent environments a certain amount of ambiguity is inevitable since no person in the organisation has clearly defined and unambiguous goals.

The Relevance of Social Learning Theory to the Development of Decision Making Skills

Jungermann (1980) speculated that we may be making decisions seem more complicated than they are by offering decision aiding systems. His conjecture

is given some support by the results reported here.
Perhaps the single most effective course of action that
can be taken by an organisation wishing to improve
its performance in decision making and problem solving,
is to examine its information processing systems to
ensure members of the organisation are not expected to
operate with unnecessarily poorly defined goals.

The most weighty support for the relevance
of social learning theory to the development of skills
in problem solving and decision making in organisations
comes from the almost universal response to question 7
in the interview data. When individuals are faced with
a challenging decision problem in which they receive
feedback on their performance, they report learning
the most significantly useful strategies for problem
solving and decision making. Subjects attributed this
learning to interaction with a significant tutor figure.
The extent to which such social learning in adults
influences cognitive strategies has not been researched
in depth. In view of the important emphasis subjects
placed on these social learning experiences, they
deserve careful investigation.

Davis and Luthans (1980) noted that organisational behaviour occurs in unique interactive sequences.
The investigation of such processes is unlikely to be
successfully undertaken using indirect questionnaire
designs for data collection. In the present study it

was not possible to explore the role that modelling plays in the development of enduring cognitive strategies. One conclusion which may be safely drawn from subjects' reports of such learning experiences, is that in each case the interaction was characterised by goal clarity.

Manz and Sims (1980) concluded that goal attainment possesses strong reinforcing properties, and would facilitate self managing behaviour. If, as Sommerhoff (1972) argued, goal directedness is an objective system property of humans, the organisation that fails to satisfy this basic human need for meaning- ful goals is in all probability wasting its resources on training in procedural rationality.

Although the literature on the effectiveness of decision training is scanty, Lichtenstein and Fischhoff (1980) found that personal and definitive feedback on performance facilitated training in probability assessment.

Bandura (1977) argued that the importance of modelling in organisational contexts had been underestimated. The present study lends weight to the argument proposed by Manz and Sims that an integration of cognitive and social learning theory provides a more powerful explanation of behaviour in organisational contexts than either theory alone.

The training referred to in this study consisted predominantly of case study methods. The

arguments summarized by Burgoyne and Stuart (1978)
in favour of Action Learning methods are consistent
with the self reports of subjects in this study.
Techniques of procedural rationality combined with
Action Learning may prove to be a more powerful
learning method than when either is used alone.
An exploration of cognitive and social learning theories
in the context of Action Learning proposed by Revans
(1971) cited in Burgoyne and Stuart (1978) offers a
promising line of enquiry toward the understanding of
human acquisition of skills for dealing with environmental complexity and uncertainty.

The assertion made by Light (1979) that
evaluation of training programs relying on interpre-
tations of surface behaviour is at best an incomplete
procedure has been substantiated in this study.
Decision making is a process of social interaction as
well as being a matter of individual judgment and
choice. There is much unexplored territory, best
suited to combined expeditionary forces of social
learning theorists and cognitive psychologists
interested in the study of individual judgment and
choice.

Phillips (1980) observed that decision
technology is more likely to be integrated into
organisational systems with a higher degree of lateral
communication. Trained subjects in this study were

critical of the decision processes characteristic
of hierarchically organised management structures.
Such structures do not encourage lateral communication
of decision making information. By directing the flow
of information through a formally organised hierarchy,
the process of decision making is highly controlled.
In stable environments this procedure is adaptive since
there is little need for new learning. In more
turbulent environments, the process of learning is
perhaps best facilitated by organisations with a greater
degree of lateral communication.

It is possible that by inhibiting new learning,
the more classical hierarchical structure of organisation in Australia Post contributed to the apparently
greater frustration among trained subjects in that
organisation. This observation is speculative as there
are several other plausible explanations, more than
one of which could be interacting with the training
to bring about a greater incidence of self reported
goal frustration. The finding is consistent with the
observations made by Phillips (1980). The suggestion
that certain forms of organisation structure may
systematically inhibit new learning requires investigation in natural settings.

Suggestions for Organisations Considering Training
in Decision Aiding

The following recommendations are suggested

for organisations considering the implementation of
training programs in decision aiding:

(1)   Ensure that key policy makers in the organisation receive and evaluate such training before proceding
further. Each organisation has unique characteristics
in its information processing system and these should
be taken into account in designing any strategy for
introducing a new "intellectual technology" into the
system.

If the policy making group are able to make
use of techniques of procedural rationality, such as
those recommended by Kepner & Tregoe (1965, 1981),
to clarify the goals of the organisation, the benefits
are likely to be significant. If the policy makers
find such techniques of little value, it is suggested
that training elsewhere in the organisation is likely
to result in more frustration than potential benefits.

(2)   The training is unlikely to be effective if
adopted piecemeal. The target population should be
one in which the members have a high degree of
interaction in their work.

(3)   The importance of coaching in structuring
decision problems cannot be overemphasized. This can
perhaps best be achieved by training respected members
of the organisation in what Janis and Mann (1977)
have described as decision counselling. Such counsellors
should be able to cross the formal boundaries within

organisational hierarchy in order to clarify policy
for those with no immediate access to the policy making
group. This process could well be the source of
valuable information for the policy making group.
This group have, by definition, the organisation's
most ill structured decisions. Without such coaching,
perhaps as an ongoing activity, training in techniques
of procedural rationality seem likely to be largely
ineffective and possibly dysfunctional.

Conclusions

Training in simple techniques of decomposition
of decision problems as a decision aid, appears to have
little systematic effect on the information processing
strategies used by individuals.

Such training appears to lead to greater dissatisfaction with lack of goal clarity in organisational
settings. The psychological salience of goal directedness in individuals appears to be a longer lasting
effect than cognitive intention to make changes in
decision behaviour.

Some evidence suggesting increased resistance
to change among trained subjects indicates they either
have more confidence in their decision rules, or are
better able to analyse the validity of objections of
important others.

"Institutionalisation" of such training
programs does not appear to produce measurably different
results.

The major weakness of the present study was the absence of pretest measures. Conclusions are therefore based on sampling inferences alone. More sensitive longitudinal study of individuals is required to establish which parts of the training are found to be most useful and why. Despite this weakness in design, it is suggested that normative theories of decision behaviour do not account for a sufficiently large proportion of variance to be useful as aids to individual decision making at their present stage of development.

Social forces appear to be the most significant factor in shaping individual decision making behaviour in organisational settings.

If the main contribution of training in decision aiding is to better communication between members of decision making groups, as appears to be the case, based on the reports of subjects in this study, there may well be less complex models capable of achieving equally useful outcomes.

Procedural rationality may not be quite the "useful fiction" for dealing with the world referred to by Morgan (1981). In truth it appears to lie somewhere in the middle, not yet fully usable, but certainly no fiction.

Reference Notes

Morris, M. J. A psychometric approach to decision
    making strategies. Unpublished manuscript, 1981.
    (Available from [9, Oak Avenue, Elsternwick,
    Victoria 3185, Australia])

Reference List

Argyris, C. Some limitations of the case method: experiences in a management development program. Academy of Management Review, 1980. 5(2), 291-298.

Armstrong, J.S., Denniston, W.B. & Gordon, M.M. The use of the decomposition principle in making judgments. Organisational Behaviour and Human Performance, 1975, 14, 257-263.

Aschenbrenner, K.M., Jaus, D. & Villani, C. Heirarchical goal structuring and pupil's job choices: testing a decision aid in the field. Acta Psychologica, 1980, 45, 35-50.

Baddeley, A. The cognitive psychology of everyday life. British Journal of Psychology, 1981, 72, 257-269.

Bar-Hillel, M. Similarity and probability. Organizational Behaviour and Human Performance, 1974, 11, 277-282

Bogart, D.H. Feedback, feedforward and feed-within: strategic information in systems. Behavioral Science, 1980, 25, 237-249.

Bandura, A. Social learning theory. Englewood-cliffs, N.J.: Prentice-Hall, 1977.

Behling, O. The case for the natural science model for research in organisational behaviour and organisation theory. Academy of Management Review, 1980, 5(4), 483-490.

Bradburn, N.M., Sudman, S. & Associates. Improving interview method and questionnaire design: response effects to threatening questions in survey research. San Francisco: Jossey Bass Inc., 1979.

Brehmer, B. In one word: not from experience. Acta Psychologica, 1980, 45, 223-246.

Burgoyne, J. & Stuart, R. Teaching and learning methods in management development. Personnel Review, 1978, 7(1), 53-58.

Cook, T.D. and Campbell, D.T. The design and conduct of quasi-experiments and true experiments in field settings. In M. Dunnette (Ed.) Handbook of industrial and organizational psychology. Chicago: Rand McNally, 1976.

Davis, T.R.V. and Luthans, F. A social learning approach to organizational behaviour. Academy of Management Review, 1980, 5(2), 281-290.

Driver, M.J. and Mock, T.J. Human information processing, decision style theory, and accounting information systems. The Accounting Review, 1975, 50, 491-508.

Dubin, R. Theory building in applied areas. In M. Dunnette (Ed.) Handbook of industrial and organisational psychology. Chicago: Rand McNally, 1976.

Easterby-Smith, M. The evaluation of management education and development: an overview. Personnel Review, 1981, 10(2), 28-36.

Einhorn, H.J. and Hogarth, R.M. Behavioral decision theory: processes of judgment and choice. Annual Review of Psychology, 1981, 32, 53-88.

Emery, F.E., & Trist, E.L. The causal texture of organisational environments. Human Relations, 1965, 18, 21-32.

Ericson, K.A. and Simon, H.A. Verbal reports as data, Psychological Review, 1980, 87, 215-251.

Galbraith, J. Designing complex organizations. Reading, MA: Addison-Wesley, 1973.

Gauld, A. and Shotter, J. Human action and its psychological investigation. London: Routledge and Kepan Paul, 1977.

Ginsberg, H. and Opper, S. Piaget's theory of intellectual development (2nd ed.). New Jersey: Prentice-Hall, Inc., 1979.

Hammond, K.R., McClelland, G.H. and Mumpower, J. Human judgment and decision making: theories, methods and procedures. New York: Praeger Publishers, 1980.

Hill, T.E. and Schmitt, N. Individual differences in leader decisions. Organisation Behaviour and Human Performance, 1977, 19, 353-367.

Hogarth, R.M. Judgment and choice. Chichester: John Wiley and Sons, 1980.

Humphreys, P. and McFadden, W. Experiences with MAUD: aiding decision structuring versus bootstrapping the decision maker. Acta Psychologica, 1980, 45, 51-70.

Janis, I.L. and Mann, L. Decision making: a psychological analysis of conflict, choice and commitment. New York: The Free Press, 1977.

Jungermann, H. Speculations about decision - theoretic aids for personal decision making. Acta Psychologica, 1980, 45, 7-34.

Kahneman, D. and Tversky, A. Subjective probability: a judgment of representativeness. Cognitive Psychology, 1972, 3, 430-454.

Kahnemann, D. and Tversky, A. The psychology of preferences. Scientific American, 1982, 246(1), 136-142.

Katz, D. and Kahn, R.L. The social psychology of organizations. New York: John Wiley, 1978.

Keeney, R.L. and Raiffa, H. Decisions with multiple objectives: preferences value tradeoffs. New York: Wiley, 1976.

Kepner, C.H. and Tregoe, B.B. The rational manager. New York: McGraw-Hill, 1965.

Kepner, C.H. and Tregoe, B.B. The new rational manager. New Jersey: Princeton Research Press, 1981.

Kuhn, T.S. The structure of scientific revolutions (2nd ed.) Chicago: The University of Chicago Press, 1962.

Lichtenstein, S. and Fischhoff, B. Training for calibration. Organizational Behavior and Human Performance, 1980, 26, 149-171.

Light, D. (Jr.) Surface data and deep structure: observing the organization of professional training. Administrative Science Quarterly, 1979, 24, 551-559.

Lyon, D. and Slovic, P. Dominance of accuracy information and neglect of base rates in probability estimation. Acta Psychologica, 1976, 40, 287-298.

Mackinnon, A.J. and Wearing, A.J. Complexity and decision making. Behavioral Science, 1980, 25, 285-296.

MacCrimmon, K.R. Descriptive aspects of team theory. Management Science, 1974, 20, 1323-1334.

MacCrimmon, K.R. and Taylor, R.N. Decision making and problem solving. In M. Dunnette (Ed.) Handbook of Industrial and Organisational Psychology. Chicago: Rand McNally, 1976.

Manz, C.C. and Sims, H.P. (Jr.) Self-management as a substitute for leadership: a social learning theory perspective. Academy of Management Review, 1980, 5(3), 361-367.

Milgram, S. Obedience to authority. New York:
     Harper & Row, 1974.

Morgan, G. Paradigms, metaphors and puzzle solving
     in organization theory. Administrative Science
     Quarterly, 1980, 25, 605-622.

Morris, P.E. Why Evans is wrong in criticizing
     introspective reports of subject strategies.
     British Journal of Psychology, 1981, 72,
     465-468.

Newell, A. and Simon, H.A. Human problem solving.
     New Jersey: Prentice-Hall, 1972.

Nisbett, R.E. and Wilson, T. De C. Telling more
     than we can know: verbal reports on mental
     processes. Psychological Review, 1977, 84(3),
     231-59.

Norman, D.A. Memory and attention: an introduc-
     tion to human information processing. New
     York: John Wiley and Sons, Inc., 1976.

Phillips, L.D. Organisational structure and
     · decision technology. Acta Psychologica,
     1980, 45, 247-264.

Piaget, J. and Inhelder, D. The child's construc-
     tion of quantities: conservation and atomism,
     trans. A.J. Pomerans, New York: Basic Books,
     Inc., 1974.

Pitz, G.F., Sachs, N.J. and Heerboth, J.
    Procedures for eliciting choices in the
    analysis of individual decisions. Organiza-
    tional Behavior and Human Performance, 1980,
    26, 396-408.

Simon, H.A. The shape of automation for men and
    management. New York: Harper & Row, 1965.

Simon, H.A. Administrative behavior, New York:
    Free Press, 1976.

Slovic, P., Fischhoff, B. and Lichtenstein, S.
    Behavioral decision theory. Annual Review
    of Psychology, 1977, 28, 1-39.

Sommerhoff, G. The abstract characteristics of
    living systems. In Emery, F.E. (Ed.)
    Systems Thinking, Harmondsworth: Penguin,
    1969.

Stokes, T.F. and Baer, D.M. An implicit
    technology of generalization. Journal of
    Applied Behavior Analysis, 1977, 10, 349-367.

Thorngate, W. Efficient decision heuristics,
    Behavioral Science, 1980, 25, 219-225.

Toda, M. Emotion and decision making. Acta
    Psychologica, 1980, 45, 133-168.

Tversky, A. A theory of choice. Psychological Review, 1972, 78, 272-299.

Tversky, A. and Kahneman, D. Judgment under uncertainty: heuristics and biases. Science, 1974, 185, 1124-1131.

Tversky, A. and Kahneman, D. Causal thinking in judgment under uncertainty. In R. Butts and J. Hintikka (Eds.), Basic problems in methodology and linguistics. Dordrecht-Holland, Reidel, 1977.

Tversky, A. and Sattath, S. Preference trees. Psychological Review, 1979, 86, 542-573.

Ungson, G.R., Braunstein, D.N., and Hall, P.D. Managerial information processing: a research review. Administrative Science Quarterly, 1981, 26, 116-134.

Van Maanen, J. Reclaiming qualitative methods for organizational research: a preface. Administrative Science Quarterly, 1979, 24, 520-527.

Winterfeldt, D. Structuring decision problems for decision analysis. Acta Psychologica, 1980 45, 71-93.

APPENDICES

Final Honours Thesis of
Martin J. Morris, Department
of Psychology, University of
Melbourne.

Comprising one part of the final
assessment for the Degree of
Bachelor of Arts (Hons).

Thesis Supervisor: Professor Alexander
Wearing

Submitted for examination
November 1982.

TABLE OF CONTENTS

Table of Contents - continued

1

APPENDIX A

Australia Post Training Evaluation

REPORT ON PILOT TRAINING PROGRAM IN
DECISION MAKING

By: E.C. Whelan
PROJECT OFFICER
TRAINING AND DEVELOPMENT

CONTENTS

:

1.   PURPOSE OF REPORT   4

1.1   The aim of this report is to evaluate the pilot training
programme on "Decision Making", conducted by Martin Morris and Associates
on behalf of Australia Post at 71 Rathdowne Street in the period between
19 November 1980 and 4 December 1980.

1.2   This evaluation is based on feedback from course participants
regarding both the course itself and more importantly the application of
the techniques taught on the job. The results obtained then being
assessed and evaluated in terms of the objectives established for the
programme.

2.   INTRODUCTION

2.1   Following strong criticism by senior management of the standard
of written communication within Australia Post, Headquarters Training
and Development Branch instigated an investigation of the causes of this
problem. This investigation was conducted by management consultants
from the Australian Institute of Management.

2.2   When the findings of the AIM investigation where considered in
conjunction with the findings of the Organisation Climate Survey, which
highlighted areas of strength and weakness in the organisation as percieved
by staff members, it became apparent that the problem with written
communication had two basic causes:-

    -    Lack of a systematic approach to problem solving when preparing
recommendations.

    -    In some cases lack of appropriate report writing skills.

2.3   In order to solve these problems it was decided that two
separate training programmes would be required, one in decision making/problem
solving techniques and one in report writing skills. It was further
decided that these programmes would be conducted initially on a pilot
basis, to enable Training and Development Branch to assess their effectiveness
in improving written communication before implementing either of them on
a full scale basis.

2.4   After extensive enquiries and investigation by Training and
Development Branch, Martin Morris and Associates where engaged to conduct
the pilot programme in Decision Making and Problem Solving Techniques.
This firm of consultants was selected because of their extensive experience
in the area of managerial problem solving and decision making and because
of the impressive record the principle of the firm (Mr Martin Morris)
had in this field of training.

3.   OBJECTIVES OF THE PROGRAMME

3.1   The need, as defined by Training and Development Branch to
Martin Morris and Associates, was to provide officers involved in the
preparation of reports to senior management with training in problem
solving and in decision making that would enable them to improve both
the standard of the recommendations made in those reports and the manner
in which the recommendations were presented.

3.2   In accord with this need Martin Morris and Associates developed the following detailed objectives for the programme.

At the end of the training, participants will be able to:-

1.   Identify their concerns and set priorities.

2.   Separate concerns into -

    a.   Problems requiring further analysis to establish cause;

    b.   Decisions to be made;

    c.   Decisions already made requiring planned implementation.

3.   Distinguish between information relevant to the problem and peripheral data. Develop techniques for probing for relevant data.

4.   Be clear about what they are trying to achieve.

5.   Specify, collect, clarify, classify, interpret and evaluate the information relevant to that purpose.

6.   Develop and evaluate alternative solutions and apply them.

7.   Plan the implementation of a chosen solution and, in so doing, avoid potential problems.

8.   Measure the results of their actions.

4.   PROGRAMME DESIGN

4.1   The pilot programme consisted of three separate courses, each course being of four days duration and conducted in two sessions of two days each, the sessions being separated by approximately 5 working days. In addition a follow up ½ day was allocated to each participant for the purposes of reinforcement and evaluation of the training by the consultant

4.2   The programme had four key components:-

    -    Problem Analysis
    -    Decision Making
    -    Potential Problem Analysis
    -    Creative Problem Solving (Synectics)

4.3   Prior to the training the senior manager, or their proxy, from each area involved was given a pre-course briefing by the consultant on the objectives, methodology and expected outcomes of the programme.

A copy of the course programme giving the detailed course content is attached at Appendix 1.

5.   COURSE PARTICIPANTS

5.1   A total of 40 officers, varying in classification from Clerk Class 6, to Manager, Level 1, from Personnel, Operations and Marketing Services, attended the programme.

5.2   The participants were selected only from branches in which it was considered that the work performed required skills in both problem solving and decision making and in which the preparation of reports was part of the normal duties. In the case of Policies and Standards Sub-Section, Field Services Branch, staff were selected at the request of their manager, Mr J. Nicholls, who believed that they had a specific need in the areas this programme covered. On investigation Training and Development agreed with this assessment by Mr Nicholls.

5.3   The Branches from which the officers came, together with the number from each area are given at Appendix 2.

6.   METHOD OF EVALUATION

6.1   To obtain the participants' views on the course and to ascertain the amount of transfer of the techniques taught to the participants' job a two-stage evaluation program was carried out.

6.2   The first stage consisted of a questionnaire, that was filled out immediately after the course ended. A copy of the questionnaire, complete with a tabulation of the responses, is attached at Appendix 3.

6.3   The second stage was a series of follow-up interviews held approximately ten weeks after the end of the programme, all available participants, including Branch and Section managers being interviewed. The aim of these interviews being to ascertain the extent to which the techniques taught on the programme were being applied on the job and their consequent impact on the standard of written reports. These interviews were conducted in an informal manner, but were based on the structured question sheet shown at Appendix 4.

7.   PARTICIPANT ATTITUDE TO THE TRAINING COURSE

7.1   Participant reaction to the training course was, with one or two exceptions, extremely favourable. The content was seen to have practical application and the general format of the course was well received. There were, however, some difficulties.

-      While a pre-course briefing was given to the Branch Managers, the lack of a similar briefing for all participants caused significant problems. A large number of participants were ill-prepared for the work-related case study and most participants went on to the course unaware of how the training could improve their performance on-the-job.

-      Some case studies were considered to be unnecessarily complex. This detracted from their value as a training tool.

-      Lack of a course handout listing the various steps required to perform each of the techniques taught. A handout would have made application of the techniques on-the-job far easier.

-      The creative problem solving technique of synectics drew a large amount of critical comment and it would appear to have less application in our present work environment than the other techniques.

- The ½ day reinforcement follow-up by Martin Morris was too short to be of much assistance to the participants. Also work projects on which the techniques could be used were not identified in all cases. These problems were compounded by the fact that a few participants, for various reasons, had not received any follow-up.

8.   APPLICATION ON THE JOB

8.1   In the ten week period between the end of the course and the evaluation interview 67% of participants claimed to have used at least one, or a major part of one, of the techniques taught by Martin Morris on the job. However, as in some cases the techniques had been used only on peripheral or secondary tasks, the number of participants who had made effective use of them was nearer to 50%. This rate of usage would probably have been greater if the programme had not finished just prior to the Christmas period.

8.2   The techniques in common use were problem solving, decision making and potential problem analysis. Synetics had, however, been used by only a small percentage of the participants and little enthusiasm was expressed regarding its potential for future application.

8.3   The interviews revealed that a number of participants had used one or two of the techniques in the period immediately after the course but had failed to use them since. The reasons given for this varied, but in most cases it boiled down to them reverting to their old work patterns out of habit, or their failing to see the applicability of the new techniques to the problems confronting them.

8.4   The work area that had by far the greatest transfer of the techniques presented on the programme to the job was Organisation Branch, where all but one of the officers trained had made some use of those techniques. The amount of use naturally varied but it is significant that all managers in the branch had used the techniques both individually and in conjunction with members of their staff and all expressed commitment of their continued use.

8.5   It was interesting to find out that of the eleven participants who claimed never to have used any of the techniques on the job seven came from Commercial Branch, Marketing Services Department. The reasons given for the lack of use in this branch show that four of the officers concerned are performing jobs whose duties do not allow for the use of these techniques, except in a fairly limited way. The reasons given for others in this Branch not applying the techniques to their jobs were lack of a clear appreciation of how and when to use them, lack of appropriate current projects and a perceived lack of management commitment

8.6   In the other areas involved, that is Training and Development Branch and Field Services Branch, the use of the techniques was fairly wide spread, at least in the period immediately after the programme. However, while some positive benefits were reported most results achieved have been unclear. One possible cause of this may have been the lack of follow up, with the associated reinforcement, by management in these branches.

8.7   When analysing the factors that caused the programme to succeed in Organisation Branch, while it had only a limited effect on the other work areas, the following factors became apparent:-

    -     Organisation Branch was the only branch from which every available officer from Branch Manager down, with the exception of the Clerical Assistants and Stenographer, attended.

    -     All managers from Organization Branch are committed to the techniques and have used them in conjunction with their staff.

    -      All staff in Organisation Branch are involved in project work that has a large problem solving/decision making component.

    -     Immediate and well publicised success was achieved by the use of the decision making technique (on the project dealing with Word Processing).

8.8   All of these factors appear to some extent to have influenced the success of the programme in Organisation Branch. However, it appears from the information gathered that the most significant were the commitment of management to the programme, which involved managers in working through various work problems with their staff using the techniques, and the training of all staff in the branch at the same time.

9.   EFFECT ON STANDARD OF WRITTEN REPORTS

9.1   All managers, whose staff were using the various techniques on the job, were asked to comment on any changes or specific improvements in the reports written by their subordinates.

9.2   The only work area that displayed any signficant change attributable to the training recieved was Organisation Branch, where all managers reported some improvement in the standard of reports written by their staff. These improvements were specifically in the way factual data was presented, the way in which key issues were identified and in the method of analysis used. Significantly this improvement was most marked in the two officers whom it was considered needed most improvement in this area.

9.3   No significant change in the standard of written reports was identified in the other work areas that had staff trained on the programme.

10. SUMMARY

10.1   In terms of achieving its specific objective, that is to train officers in decision making and problem solving techniques, the pilot programme achieved mixed results. In Organisation Branch results show that this objective has to a large extent been successfully met whereas results elsewhere have at best been unclear.

10.2   The successful use of the Decision Making, Problem Solving and Potential Problem Analysis techniques in Organisation Branch has demonstrat that these techniques are both practical and relevant to the problems of Australia Post. There was, however, no similar evidence to support the value of Synectics.

10.3   It is significant that when comparing the results obtained to the prime objective of this programme, that is to improve the standard of written reports, that only Organisation Branch reported a noticeable improvement in this area. From this it can be concluded that the technique will improve the standard of written reports, but only if they are actively applied on the job as the key step in the problem solving and decision making processes, as they have been in Organisation Branch but not elsewhere.

10.4   The major difficulty encountered with the pilot programme, in areas other than Organisation Branch, was in getting participants to apply the techniques learnt to their own job. Analysis of the reasons for Organisation Branches success in this area shows that the probability of achieving transfer to the job is greatly enhanced if a work area is trained as a complete unit and if the managers of that area have a commitment to the use of the techniques.

10.5   The fact that many officers used the techniques once or twice and then reverted to their old methods, together, with the number who claimed still not to fully comprehend how or when to apply the various techniques, indicate the need for a more extensive course follow-up than that provided in the pilot programme.

11. CONCLUSION

11.1   The need for extensive reinforcement action after the initial training was the most significant finding of the evaluation. The reinforcement required can be divided into two areas of responsibility. Firstly, the follow up by the training consultant, required to assist the participants with practical difficulties encountered in applying the techniques to the job and to help identify areas of potential application for the participants. Secondly, and most importantly, the reinforcement provided by the participants manager. For it would appear that the managers attitude to the techniques, together with the managers willingness to investigate a problem by the use of these techniques in conjunction with his/her staff, was of paramount importance in the successful transfer of the techniques to the work situation.

11.2   It is therefore apparent that before any future training programme is implemented a comprehensive follow up programme be devised for the trainer/consultant and commitment be obtained from the relevant managers that they will provide the necessary on the job reinforcement for their staff.

11.3   From the nature of the projects that the techniques have been successfully applied to, it appears that use of the techniques is both more likely and the results obtained: more apparent when the project concerned has clearly defined objectives and can be completed in a comparatively short time span. In the future better results may therefore be obtained from the training, if participants are able, immediately after the training course, to work on a project that they can control from start to finish and that has specific objectives.

11.4   The results of the evaluation indicate that the training course would be more successful, in terms of transfer to the work face, if the following steps were taken.

-     Provide a briefing on course objectives and requirements to all participants before the course.

-     Delete synectics.

-     Remove unnecessary complexities from case studies.

-     Provide a handout summarizing the techniques at the end of the course.

11.5   The inclusion of some officers on the programme who did not have a clearly job related need for this training demonstrates a weakness in the current method for accepting course nominations. In the future Training and Development will have to take even greater care when both seeking and accepting nominations, to ensure that only officers with a demonstrable need are sent on courses of this type by their managers.

12. RECOMMENDATIONS

12.1   It is recommended that we proceed with a training programme based on the pilot programme, but modified in light of the findings of this report and limited to those areas that have a clearly demonstrated need for this type of training.

12.2   Before commencing the new programme Training and Development first determine areas that have a need for this training, and then obtain agreement from the management of the areas identified that all officers in that area performing relevant duties, including all managers, will receive the training.

12.3   A comprehensive follow up programme be implemented after the training course to ensure the transfer of the techniques to the job. This follow-up to consist of two elements:

-     Reinforcement by the appropriate managers, in that they encourage their staff to use the techniques and when appropriate use the techniques in conjunction with their staff.

-     A three months follow-up period during which the trainer/ consultant will on a regular basis discuss the application of the techniques to the participant's job, highlight areas of potential use and assist with any difficulties encountered.

Day 1

8.30   Introduction to the processes of Problem Solving and Decision Making.

9.15   Discussions and clarification of programme objectives in end result terms.

9.30   The key processes in each of the following critical areas:

         1.   Situation Analysis;

         2.   Priority Setting;

         3.   Problem Analysis;

         4.   Decision Making;

         5.   Planning and Potential Problem Analysis.

10.30   Morning Tea

10.45   Case Study to analyse your highest priority concerns.

11.45   Case Study feedback.

12.15   Lunch.

1.00   Problem Analysis Step by Step using a 2 part Case Study.

2.30   Afternoon Tea.

2.45   Group application of Problem Analysis to Case Study in syndicates.

4.00   Case Study feedback and reinforcement of learning.

4.30   Identify own problems and begin to specify the data required to analyse the problem.

5.00   Finish.

Day 2

8.30   Introduction to Decision Making Processes:

        Review different types of Decision - Adaptive;
                                              Interim;
                                              Corrective;

9.30   Individual and Group Decision Making exercise.

10.30   Morning Tea.

10.45   Review of Decision Making exercise.

11.15   Steps in Rational Decision Making.

11.45   Case Study to set objectives for first decision.

12.45   Lunch.

1.30   Syndicates to practise techniques of Decision Analysis
        on Case Study as far as tentative Decision.

2.15   Review Case Study.

2.45   Afternoon Tea.

3.00   Analysis of Adverse Consequences and Potential Problem
        Analysis.

4.00   Syndicates to complete Case Study.

5.00   Finish.

Day 3

8.30   Creative thinking and its application in decision making.

                 1.   Generating alternatives;

                 2.   Synetics approach to problem solving/decision making.

10.00   Morning Tea

10.15   Synetics Approach.

11.15   Syndicate practice on own problems.

12.15   Lunch.

1.00   Syndicates to apply techniques learned so far to own situations with guidance from trainer.

5.00   Finish.

Day 4

8.30   Potential Problem Analysis in Planning.

9.30   Case Study in Potential Problem Analysis.

10.30   Morning Tea.

10.45   For the remainder of the day syndicates will work on own
            problems under the supervision of the trainer. The
            trainer will spend time with each individual during the
            afternoon clarifying material and its relevance to your
            own position in Australia Post.

COURSE PARTICIPANTS

The work areas from which the officers came, together with the number from each area were as follows:

Personnel Department

Organisation Branch - 13
Training and Development - 8

Operations Department

Field Services Branch
    Policies and Standards   Section-6

Marketing Services Department

Commercial Branch
    Charges and Agencies Section - 4
    Market Plan and Research Section - 4
    Customer Services Section - 4

DECISION MAKING TECHNIQUES PROGRAMME - EVALUATION
STAGE I

$N = 35$

Having completed the course do you think it was

1. Circle one number

    1. A very good idea   17
    2. A fairly good idea   18
    3. Neither   —
    4. A fairly bad idea   — $\bar{x} = 1.5$
    5. A very bad idea   —

How interesting has the course been?

2. Circle one number

    1. Very interesting   15
    2. Fairly interesting   19
    3. Neither   1 $\bar{x} = 1.6$
    4. Not very interesting   —
    5. Not at all interesting —

How useful do you feel the course will be to you in your job?

3. Circle one number

    1. Very useful   11
    2. Fairly useful   23 $\bar{x} = 1.7$
    3. Neither   —
    4. Not very useful   1
    5. Not at all useful   —

If you feel it will be either "not very" or "not at all useful", please
say why.

4. Do you expect any changes in your work behaviour as a result of
    this course?

    NONE   1   2   3   4   5   6   7   SUBSTANTIAL $\bar{x} = 4.3$

    Specify possible changes, if any :

5. List in order the elements of the course you found of most value :

    1. ....
        ....

    2. ....
        ....

    3. ....
        ....

6. List in order the elements of the course you found of least value :

    1. ....
        ....

    2. ....
        ....

    3. ....
        ....

7. How would you rate the duration of the following?

Circle one number for each item	TOO LONG	ABOUT RIGHT	TOO SHO
The course overall	1 1	2 /3	3
The length of the day	1 9	2 2(	3
The breaks for meals, coffee etc	1 2	2 30	3
Case study work	1 /2	2 /5	3
Syndicate work	1 (	2 23	3

8. How much value to you was

	LITTLE VALUE	MEDIUM VALUE	HIC VAL
Day one (problem analysis)	1 3	2 /3	3
Day two (decision making process)	1 NIL	2 9	3
Day three (creative/thinking/synectics)	1 /3	2 /5	3
Day four (potential problems/your problem)	1 5	2 /5	3

9. If there were any particular elements of the course which - in your opinion - need considerable improvement, please say which they were, and why improvements need to be made.

10. Would you like further training in decision making/problem solving?

 Yes 22   No 13

 If possible specify area or type of extra training :

11. Are there any comments or suggestions you would like to make?

DECISION MAKING COURSE - EVALUATION - STAGE 2

NAME ....   DATE ....

1. Have you applied the skills learnt:

    a. Problem Analysis   Yes/No

    b. Decision Making   Yes/No

    c. Potential Problem Analysis   Yes/No

    d. Synetics   Yes/No

2. If not - why?

3. If yes - How successful? - results obtained (examples)

4. Do you have any suggestions for course improvement?

5. In which areas of Australia Post should this course be given?

6. General Comments.

ANALYSIS OF COURSE CONTENT

In general the response to the content of the first two days of the course, that is problem analysis and decision making, was extremely favourable. Whereas, the response to the content of the third and fourth days of the course was less favourable with "Synectics" in particular drawing much negative comment.

Problem Solving - Immediately after the course 54% of participants felt Problem Analysis to be high value to themselves and only 8% felt it to be of little value. Amongst those people who have since used this technique on the job responses have in most cases been very favourable.

> "I have been able to get people to recognise the real problems, in the past this was hard".

However, in a number of cases comments were made about the process employed in problem solving being confusing or difficult to use.

> "Can still get lost when using it".

These responses may indicate that more time is required for people to reach competence in this technique than was allowed on the pilot programme.

Decision Making - Immediately after the course 75% of participants felt this to be a high value to themselves whereas none rated it as being of little value. This is an exceptionally positive response. The follow up interviews revealed that most participants who had used this technique were happy with the results.

> "Really like the idea of Musts and Wants".

> "Has been helpful, it identifies areas of dispute".

However, once again some found the technique too complex for common usage.

> "Very cumbersome, the large number of steps is a bit off putting - its hard to remember".

Others felt that the technique was best suited for use in project groups and may not be really useful on individual work.

> "Process appears to work better with a group, if you do it by yourself the formal steps tend to slow you down".

These responses may indicate that the decision making technique is currently to complex for use on simple problems or for use by officers working in isolation. We may therefore have to investigate ways of overcoming these objections in any future training.

Synectics - Immediately after the course only 26% of participants felt this to be a high value, while 37% felt it to be of low value. This resonse was reinforced by the fact that 15 participants listed Synectics as one of the elements of least value. This attitude was still apparent during the evaluation interviews, when only two comments were made in favour of synectics and at least 30% of those interviewed made comments against it.

"Synectics distrubs me a little, I cannot bring myself to act in this manner".

"Synectics damages the credibility of the reas of the course".

The strength and frequency of these responses indicates that we should look carefully at synectics in the context of the current climate within Australia Post, Headquarters.

Potential Problem Analysis - As this technique took up only a short period on either the third or the fourth day of the course a detailed analysis of participants response to it is not possible. This technique also aroused little interest during the evaluation interviews, perhaps as a result of the short time alloted to it on the course.

Case Studies - Most participants interviewed saw the case studies given as a vital ingredient of the training. But a number did express reservatio about certain features of the case studies mainly the length and complexity of some of them.

"Would like more and shorter case studies to given extra practice".

"Initial case studies too complicated, would have benefited from less complex ones".

"More but shorter case studies".

The frequency of these comments indicates that the case studies used may need to be reviewed before any future training is given. In particular all irrelevant detail should be deleted from the case studies, even in this requries the listing of relevant factors in point form.

An interesting factor which came out of the evaluation interviews was that some of the participants felt their real difficulty was with the lack of clear objectives given to them for a project.

"Biggest problem is to get clients/managers to define their problems and expectations".

These responses indicate that the elements of the course that deal with objective setting and objective clarification need to be strengthend to overcome this problem.

APPENDIX B

(1)   Decision Making Questionnaire

(2)   Information Processing Style Inventory

(3)   Cognitive Activities Inventory

(4)   Model of Decision Making Processes

(5)   Eight Questions forming the Interview Structure

(6)   Details of the content of the Training Program

(7)   Brief Synopsis of responses to Question 7 in
        the Interviews

(8)   Detailed Reliability Data for Decision Making
        Questionnaire

DECISION MAKING QUESTIONNAIRE

Thank you for participating in this study. Since each
individual has his or her own unique tastes, preferences
and decision style, there cannot be "right" or "wrong"
answers to the questions and statements that follow.
The aim of the study is to explore the ways people
experience uncertainty which is a feeling we all share
to some degree when making decisions.

As with any questionnaire, there will be occasions when
none of the available responses fits exactly with the
way you generally feel when making decisions. In these
cases, please give the response that most closely
corresponds with the way you view your position.

At the end of the questionnaire space is provided for
you to make any comments you wish concerning your own
personal experience of uncertainty in decision making.
Your comments will be both helpful and appreciated.

All questionnaires are coded to protect the anonymity
of respondents. Once your completed questionnaire is
received and your responses are combined with others from
your organisation, the questionnaire submitted by you will
be destroyed. Summarized results will be available to all
participants at the completion of the study.

Once again, thank you for giving your time to help in
this project. It is hoped that the results will prove
useful in further understanding the processes of decision
making in organisations.

When responding to items in the questionnaire, please
circle the item number: e.g.

1
2
3
4
5

1. THE EXTENT TO WHICH I HAVE CONFIDENCE IN
   MY DECISIONS

   1   Very confident always
   2   Often confident
   3   Fairly confident
   4   Occasionally confident
   5   Not at all confident

2. I KICK MYSELF FOR NOT ACTING MORE QUICKLY

   1   Very frequently
   2   Quite frequently
   3   More than occasionally
   4   Occasionally
   5   Very rarely

3. MY DECISION MAKING IS OVERTAKEN BY EVENTS

   1   Very frequently
   2   Quite frequently
   3   More than occasionally
   4   Occasionally
   5   Very rarely

4. I LIKE TO SLEEP ON IT BEFORE COMMITTING
   MYSELF TO AN IMPORTANT DECISION

   1   Always
   2   Almost always
   3   More than occasionally
   4   Occasionally
   5   Very rarely or never

5. I AVOID MAKING DECISIONS THAT REQUIRE
   COMMITMENT

   1   Very frequently
   2   Quite frequently
   3   More than occasionally
   4   Occasionally
   5   Very rarely or never

6. COOPERATING WITH OTHERS IN THE PROCESS OF
   PROBLEM SOLVING AND DECISION MAKING IS FOR ME

   1   Always easy
   2   Usually easy
   3   Occasionally difficult
   4   Often difficult
   5   Always difficult

7. THE FREQUENCY WITH WHICH I CHANGE MY MIND
   WITHOUT BEING AWARE OF THE REASON IS

   1   Very frequently
   2   Quite frequently
   3   More than occasionally
   4   Occasionally
   5   Very rarely

8. MY TECHNIQUES FOR QUESTIONING OTHER PEOPLE
    TO OBTAIN INFORMATION CONCERNING PROBLEMS ARE

    1   Highly specific and systematic
    2   Somewhat searching and systematic
    3   Sometimes systematic
    4   Determined by my previous experience
    5   Determined by the particular problem

9. THE EXTENT TO WHICH I AM CONFIDENT OF MY
    ABILITY TO JUDGE PROBABILITIES OF FUTURE
    EVENTS AFFECTING MY DECISIONS

    1   Very confident always
    2   Often confident
    3   Fairly confident
    4   Occasionally confident
    5   Not at all confident

10. WHEN MAKING IMPORTANT DECISIONS I OVERLOOK
    POTENTIALLY GOOD ALTERNATIVES

    1   Always
    2   Almost always
    3   More often than not
    4   Sometimes
    5   Rarely or never

11. THE EXTENT TO WHICH I GENERALLY FEEL THE
    OUTCOMES OF MY DECISIONS ARE WITHIN MY CONTROL

    1   Almost entirely within my control
    2   Quite considerably within my control
    3   Just within my control
    4   To some extent outside my control
    5   Very much outside my control

12. I TRY TO CONSIDER EVERY ALTERNATIVE BEFORE
    MAKING A DECISION

    1   Always
    2   Almost always
    3   More often than not
    4   Sometimes
    5   Rarely or never

13. ORGANISING RELEVANT INFORMATION CONCERNING
    A PROBLEM OR DECISION IS A PROCEDURE I
    FIND

    1   Very easy to accomplish
    2   Usually easy to accomplish
    3   Occasionally difficult to accomplish
    4   Often difficult to accomplish
    5   Very difficult to accomplish

14. I EXPERIENCE DIFFICULTY IN MAKING COMPARISONS
    BETWEEN POSSIBLE ALTERNATIVES

    1   Very frequently
    2   Quite frequently
    3   More than occasionally
    4   Occasionally
    5   Very rarely or never

15. DIFFICULT DECISIONS SEEM TO ME HOPELESS TO
    RESOLVE SATISFACTORILY

    1   Very frequently
    2   Quite frequently
    3   More than occasionally
    4   Occasionally
    5   Very rarely or never

16. I MAKE DECISIONS EASILY

    1   Always
    2   Almost always
    3   More often than not
    4   Sometimes
    5   Rarely or never

17. I EXPERIENCE UNCOMFORTABLE FEELINGS OF
    UNCERTAINTY WHEN MAKING IMPORTANT DECISIONS

    1   Always
    2   Almost always
    3   More often than not
    4   Sometimes
    5   Rarely or never

18. I FIND MYSELF BROODING OVER DECISIONS

    1   Very frequently
    2   Quite frequently
    3   More than occasionally
    4   Occasionally
    5   Very rarely

19. THE OUTCOMES OF MY DECISIONS WOULD BE MORE
    SATISFACTORY IF I ALLOWED MORE TIME FOR
    DECISION MAKING

    1   Very frequently
    2   Quite frequently
    3   More than occasionally
    4   Occasionally
    5   Very rarely

20. EFFECTIVENESS IN DECISION MAKING AND PROBLEM
    SOLVING IS A SKILL THAT CAN BE SYSTEMATICALLY
    DEVELOPED WITH APPROPRIATE TRAINING

    1   Strongly agree
    2   Generally agree
    3   Can't be sure
    4   Generally disagree
    5   Strongly disagree

21. COMMUNICATING WITH OTHER PEOPLE IS A
    SOURCE OF DIFFICULTY FOR ME IN THE PROCESS
    OF PROBLEM SOLVING AND DECISION MAKING

    1   Only occasionally
    2   Sometimes
    3   More often than not
    4   Almost always
    5   Always

22. THE IMPORTANCE OF PERSONAL INTUITION IN MY
    OWN DECISION MAKING IS

    1   Of very great importance indeed
    2   Of quite considerable importance
    3   Of some importance
    4   Of little importance
    5   Very insignificant importance

23. THE FREQUENCY WITH WHICH I FEEL UNSURE OF
    WHAT I WANT FROM A DECISION

    1   I very frequently feel unsure
    2   I quite frequently feel unsure
    3   I more than occasionally feel unsure
    4   I occasionally feel unsure
    5   I very seldom feel unsure

24. I AM FORCED TO MAKE HASTY DECISIONS

    1   Very frequently
    2   Quite frequently
    3   More than occasionally
    4   Occasionally
    5   Very rarely

25. CONSIDERATION OF DETAILED INFORMATION
    RELATING TO ALTERNATIVE COURSES OF ACTION IS

    1   Of very great importance indeed
    2   Of quite considerable importance
    3   Of some importance
    4   Of little importance
    5   Very insignificant importance

26. IMPORTANT DECISIONS CAUSE ME TO FEEL
    ANXIOUS

    1   Very frequently
    2   Quite frequently
    3   More than occasionally
    4   Occasionally
    5   Very rarely or never

27. THERE ARE TIMES WHEN I FEEL I JUST CANNOT
    MAKE A DECISION

    1   Very frequently
    2   Quite frequently
    3   More than occasionally
    4   Occasionally
    5   Very rarely or never

28. I LEAVE DECISIONS UNTIL THE LAST
OPPORTUNITY

    1   Very frequently
    2   Quite frequently
    3   More than occasionally
    4   Occasionally
    5   Very rarely or never

29. THE EXTENT TO WHICH I AM SATISFIED WITH MY
ABILITY TO COLLECT AND ORGANISE RELEVANT
INFORMATION FOR MY DECISIONS

    1   Very satisfied
    2   Generally satisfied
    3   Occasionally dissatisfied
    4   Quite often dissatisfied
    5   Very dissatisfied

30. HOW SATISFIED ARE YOU WITH THE AMOUNT OF
TIME YOU SPEND SOLVING PROBLEMS, MAKING
DECISIONS AND PLANNING

    1   Very dissatisfied, I spend too much time
    2   Unsatisfied quite often
    3   Occasionally unsatisfied
    4   Generally satisfied
    5   Very satisfied, I have all the time I
         need for other activities

31. I POSTPONE MAKING DIFFICULT DECISIONS

    1   Always
    2   Almost always
    3   More often than not
    4   Sometimes
    5   Very rarely or never

32. THE EXTENT TO WHICH I FEEL SATISFIED WITH
MY ABILITY TO HELP OTHERS WITH THEIR
DECISIONS AND PROBLEMS

    1   Very satisfied
    2   Generally satisfied
    3   Occasionally dissatisfied
    4   Quite often dissatisfied
    5   Very dissatisfied

33. I ABIDE BY MY DECISIONS

    1   Always
    2   Almost always
    3   More often than not
    4   Sometimes
    5   Rarely or never

34.   GATHERING RELEVANT INFORMATION PRIOR TO
      MAKING AN IMPORTANT DECISION IS

      1   Almost always very difficult
      2   Frequently very difficult
      3   Sometimes very difficult
      4   Occasionally very difficult
      5   Never very difficult

35.   THE EXTENT TO WHICH I FEEL SATISFIED WITH
      THE CONSISTENCY OF MY DECISION MAKING

      1   Very dissatisfied
      2   Quite often dissatisfied
      3   Occasionally dissatisfied
      4   Generally satisfied
      5   Very satisfied

36.   SOME PEOPLE ARE JUST BORN BETTER AT
      DECISION MAKING

      1   Strongly disagree
      2   Generally disagree
      3   Can't be sure
      4   Generally agree
      5   Strongly agree

37.   I GENERALLY FIND WORKING WITH OTHER PEOPLE
      ON DECISION MAKING TASKS

      1   Very frustrating and prefer working
           alone
      2   Of little help in arriving at a decision
      3   Of some help at times
      4   Usually useful in arriving at a decision
      5   Very stimulating and helpful

38.   I AM CONFIDENT THAT I AM WORKING ON THE
      MOST APPROPRIATE PROBLEM

      1   Always
      2   Almost always
      3   Usually
      4   Sometimes
      5   Only occasionally

39.   HOW SATISFIED ARE YOU GENERALLY WITH THE
      TIME IT TAKES YOU TO MAKE DECISIONS

      1   Very satisfied
      2   Generally satisfied
      3   Occasionally unsatisfied
      4   Unsatisfied quite often
      5   Very unsatisfied

40. OTHER PEOPLE'S EXPECTATIONS INFLUENCE
    MY DECISIONS

    1   To a very great extent
    2   To a large extent
    3   To some extent
    4   In small ways
    5   Hardly, if at all

41. RECOGNISING THE EARLY SIGNS OF DEVELOPING
    PROBLEMS BEFORE THEY BEGIN TO BE SERIOUS
    IS FOR ME

    1   Almost always easy
    2   Usually easy
    3   Occasionally difficult
    4   Often difficult
    5   Almost always difficult

42. I MAKE DECISIONS VERY QUICKLY

    1   Always
    2   Almost always
    3   More often than not
    4   Sometimes
    5   Rarely or never

43. I WORRY A LOT ABOUT IMPORTANT DECISIONS

    1   Always
    2   Almost always
    3   More often than not
    4   Sometimes
    5   Rarely or never

44. I CAREFULLY PLAN THE IMPLEMENTATION OF MY
    DECISIONS

    1   Always
    2   Almost always
    3   More often than not
    4   Sometimes
    5   Rarely or never

45. DECISIONS MADE IN HASTE GIVE RISE TO
    SUBSEQUENT REGRET

    1   Always
    2   Almost always
    3   More often than not
    4   Sometimes
    5   Rarely or never

46. WHEN WORKING WITH OTHERS, DEVELOPING SOLUTIONS
TO PROBLEMS, I GENERALLY FEEL

1   Very confident making suggestions for
     new approaches
2   Quite confident putting new ideas forward
3   Sometimes feel confident enough to make
     suggestions
4   Very rarely make suggestions
5   More comfortable if others take the
     lead

47. WHAT APPEARS AT FIRST TO BE THE BEST COURSE
OF ACTION IS SUBSEQUENTLY REJECTED BY ME AS
INADEQUATE

1   Always
2   Almost always
3   More often than not
4   Sometimes
5   Rarely or never

48. CREATIVITY HAS LITTLE TO DO WITH EFFECTIVE
DECISION MAKING

1   Strongly agree
2   Generally agree
3   Can't be sure
4   Generally disagree
5   Strongly disagree

49. THE FREQUENCY WITH WHICH MY DECISION OUTCOMES
ARE DETERMINED BY CHANCE FACTORS IS

1   Very frequently
2   Quite frequently
3   More than occasionally
4   Occasionally
5   Very rarely

50. A CERTAIN AMOUNT OF CONFLICT IS INEVITABLE
AND ARGUABLY USEFUL IN ORGANISATIONAL
PROBLEM SOLVING

1   Strongly agree
2   Inclined to agree
3   Don't know
4   Inclined to disagree
5   Strongly disagree

51. FOR ME, DECIDING WHICH PROBLEM TO TACKLE NEXT IS

1   Almost always difficult
2   Often difficult
3   Occasionally difficult
4   Usually easy
5   Almost always easy

52. WHEN CONFRONTED WITH A NEW AND UNFAMILIAR
     PROBLEM SITUATION I EXPERIENCE UNCOMFORTABLE
     FEELINGS OF UNCERTAINTY

     1   Always
     2   Almost always
     3   More often than not
     4   Sometimes
     5   Only occasionally

53. OTHERWISE GOOD ALTERNATIVES WHICH ARE IN
     CONFLICT WITH THE WISHES OF IMPORTANT OTHERS

     1   Are almost always readily rejected
     2   Are often rejected for this reason
     3   Are regularly but not frequently
          rejected for this reason
     4   Only occasionally rejected for this
          reason
     5   Are never rejected for this reason alone

54. WHEN MAKING IMPORTANT DECISIONS, BEFORE
     MAKING A FINAL CHOICE I FEEL

     1   Always very uncertain
     2   Frequently very uncertain
     3   Sometimes very uncertain
     4   Occasionally very uncertain
     5   Never very uncertain

55. I ARRANGE DECISION MAKING INFORMATION IN A
     LOGICAL ORDER PRIOR TO MAKING A DECISION

     1   Always
     2   Almost always
     3   More often than not
     4   Sometimes
     5   Rarely or never

56. WHEN MAKING IMPORTANT LONG TERM DECISIONS
     THE MOST DIFFICULT PART OF THE PROCESS FOR ME
     IS

     1   Knowing clearly what I want from the
          decision
     2   Obtaining relevant information about
          alternative courses of action
     3   Knowing when I have sufficient information
          to make a choice
     4   Overcoming the inertia associated with
          continuing the present course of action
     5   Making a commitment to a new course of
          action

57. WITH SOME DECISION PROBLEMS THERE IS SO MUCH
     INFORMATION AVAILABLE IT IS DIFFICULT TO
     PROCESS IT ALL. I FIND MYSELF IN THIS SITUATION

     1   Very frequently
     2   Quite frequently
     3   More than occasionally
     4   Occasionally
     5   Very rarely or never

Your comments are invited on any aspect of decision making or problem solving in conditions of uncertainty.

Information Processing Style Inventory

(1)   (a) Is it more likely that you would overlook
       possible adverse consequences when making
       decisions, or:
       (b) change your mind after making an
       important decision.

(2)   (a) Change your mind after making an important
       decision, or:
       (b) experience feelings of conflict leading
       to inertia and anxiety concerning change.

(3)   (a) Change your mind after making an important
       decision, or:
       (b) attempt to take too much information into
       account in making a decision and get overloaded.

(4)   (a) Attempt to take too much information
       into account in making a decision and get
       overloaded, or:
       (b) put off an unpleasant decision.

(5)   (a) Jump to conclusions prematurely in your
       decision making, or:
       (b) attempt to take too much information into
       account in making a decision and get overloaded.

(6)   (a) Change your mind after making an important
       decision, or:
       (b) jump to conclusions prematurely in your
       decision making.

(7)   (a) Attempt to take too much information into account in making a decision and get overloaded, or:

(b) overlook possible adverse consequences when making decisions.

(8)   (a) Experience feelings of conflict leading to inertia and anxiety concerning change, or:

(b) overlook possible adverse consequences when making decisions.

(9)   (a) Jump to conclusions prematurely in your decision making, or:

(b) overlook possible adverse consequences when making decisions.

(10)   (a) Put off an unpleasant decision, or:

(b) experience feelings of conflict, leading to inertia and anxiety concerning change.

(11)   (a) Experience feelings of conflict, leading to inertia, and anxiety concerning change, or:

(b) jump to conclusions prematurely in your decision making.

(12)   (a) Attempt to take too much information . into account in making a decision and get overloaded, or:

(b) Experience feelings of conflict leading to inertia, and anxiety concerning change.

(13)   (a) Put off an unpleasant decision, or:

         (b) jump to conclusions prematurely in your
         decision making.

(14)   (a) Change your mind after making an important
         decision, or:

         (b) put off an unpleasant decision.

(15)   (a) Overlook possible adverse consequences
         when making decisions, or:

         (b) put off an unpleasant decision.

COGNITIVE ACTIVITIES INVENTORY

CONSIDER THE FOLLOWING MENTAL ACTIVITIES
AND RANK THEM FROM MOST DIFFICULT FOR YOU
PERSONALLY TO LEAST DIFFICULT

A.   LONG RANGE PLANNING

B.   PLANNING YOUR ROUTINE, WEEK TO WEEK
     ACTIVITIES IN ORDER TO ACHIEVE SHORT
     TERM OBJECTIVES

C.   KEEPING TRACK OF ALL THE RELEVANT
     INFORMATION YOU NEED TO MAKE SHORT
     RANGE DECISIONS

D.   ANALYZING COMPLEX INTERRELATED PROBLEMS

E.   COMING UP WITH NOVEL AND WORKABLE
     SOLUTIONS TO WORK PROBLEMS

A SIMPLIFIED BUT USEFUL MODEL OF
THE COMPONENTS OF DECISION PROBLEMS

FEED FORWARD : DETERMINES
REALISTIC GOALS

GOALS

OUTCOMES OF
DECISIONS AND ACTION
DESIRED STATES OF
THE WORLD : WHERE
WE'RE HEADED

TRANSFORMATION
PROCESSES

PROBLEM SOLVING

DECISION MAKING

PLANNING

ACTIVITIES

TOWARDS GOALS

GIVENS

INFORMATION : KNOWLEDGE
OF STATES OF THE
WORLD OUT THERE :
PERSONAL "SMALL"
WORLD INSIDE

FEEDBACK ABOUT OUTCOMES
AND PROCESSES ADDS TO KNOWLEDGE

APPENDIX B

Sample of Interview Questions and Responses

*Note Responses randomly selected

Question 1. What do you think is the single biggest problem you have in decision making?

Lack of confidence in the goals. These seem to be hard to pin down and this tendency is increasing. (male manager).

Question 2. Tell me about the things that create most difficulty for you in problem solving and decision making?

As a result of having more data I seem to be becoming less certain. There is more information to process. We seem to be living in a more complex, stretched environment of decision making. The benefits of increasing technology are not flowing to information processing. (Female, graduate, senior professional).

Question 3. What are the critical external variables affecting the way you make your decisions?

Policies of the organisation and variances between my view and theirs. Often the policy is ill defined and rarely gives real guidance for my decision making. Fortunately I mostly implement other people's decisions, this is frustrating, but I don't carry the can. Decision making in this

Appendix B - continued

organisation is too centralized, we are treated
like ignorant morons, so we just do as we are told.
(Male, supervisor, graduate).

Question 4. Do you find it useful to break decisions
down into smaller components? If so, how do you do it?

I have always operated on an abbreviated
version of what you suggested we should do. Specifying the objectives before leaping into evaluating
alternatives is most useful. It all gets back to
facing up to the decision though. Once you have
confronted the goals it is relatively easy. (Trained
manager, graduate, senior position).

Question 5. If you were asked to explain your own
decision making process, how would you explain it?

Generally difficult to explain. I try to
get relevant information, sort it, rank it. Look
carefully at the objectives, try and establish
baselines. Often it just happens without me being
aware of how I arrived at a conclusion, then I worry
that I am just being expedient, taking the line of
least resistance.

Question 6. Could you tell me about your experiences
of uncertainty. When you feel uncertain, what seems
to cause it, what do you do to minimise uncertainty?

I experience uncertainty quite often at work.

Appendix B - continued

Not so much in my private life. Technology is changing faster than I can develop the ability to process change. This creates an increasing load on my capacity. I just switch off and wait for normal service to be resumed. (Male, trained, graduate).

Question 7. What do you feel has contributed most to your ability as a problem solver and decision maker? Can you point to specific experiences and describe them?

Formal education: an interest in problem solving. What is rationality? e.g. in economics. Self awareness exercises to overcome feelings of inadequacy. Coming into a planning job has compelled me to put my ideas to the test. The intellectual stimulation gained from creating something new, e.g. a new policy strategy. The creative rather than the procedural. I'm turned on by what I am doing now. Part of it is having the freedom of discretion given to me by a boss who is receptive to new ideas. He is a stimulating person who gives me a feeling of self worth, a feeling that what I am doing is being recognised. My MBA was stimulating. Now the intellectrual freedom I had then is being challenged. (Male, untrained, senior professional).

Appendix B - continued

Question 8. How do you know when you are ready to
make a decision that requires commitment?

When things fall into place. Most of the time
it just requires a leap into the unknown, then I
just make sure I am taking the least risky and
dangerous path. Often I am not committed anyway.
There are very few irreversible decisions when you
think about it. (Male, trained, middle manager).

PROBLEM SOLVING & DECISION MAKING WITHIN ORGANISATIONS

INTRODUCTION

In addition to the work of behavioural scientists, there is an extensi
literature on problem solving and decision making, comprising contributio
from mathematics, statistics, economics and politics. The focus of this pap
is not to discuss the merits and demerits of particular theoretical approach
in terms of their ultimate validity, but to examine instead a model which ler
itself to observation and analysis; to provide a conceptual framework f
problem solving and decision making within organisations; and to shift t
focus from a consideration of what problem solving and decision making is
one in which the emphasis on or the why and how of making decisions and solvi
problems.

The steps or stages in each process are considered applicable whether t
process is being used by an individual, a dyad, a small group a committee or
total organisation and in all cases this discussion assumes that they are bei
used to produce specific managerial conclusions, within the boundaries of
organisation.

To provide a conceptual overview without unnecessarily lengthening t
discussion, the integrative function of problem solving and decision maki
process within an organisation is depicted diagrammatically in Fig. 1 append
1. Additionally, each of the five analytic process under discussion, conce
analysis problem analysis, decision analysis, solution development a
potential problem analysis is presented in flow chart form in Appendices
through 6.

The systems frame of reference implicit in these flowcharts and in the rest
the paper, conceptualises a manager as an information processor. That is, he
purposively processing information pertaining to some concern for which he
responsible, in order to arrive at a specific conclusion. He is also assum
to be a communicator, actively seeking out information from his environment
both direct observation and through interaction with others.

In this paper, the emphasis is on the rationality of managerial decision maki
and problem solving behaviour. This simplifying assumption is adopted in or
to facilitate the discussion; however in a further paper which examines
psychological barriers in decision making a more complex model of man
implicit and hopefully this redresses the imbalance inherent in focussing
the three objectives discussed in the opening paragraph.

DISCUSSION

A.   Concern Analysis (Problem Finding) Overview and Rationale

A basic task of a manager is to appraise his job environment and to separate out from it those aspects of the situation which require further thought or processing. It is also necessary to get clear about which of these concerns have the highest priority, since he can only work on one item at a time, and also he has to select for each separate concern an appropriate reasoning process which will enable him to reach to process it until he has arrived at an appropriate conclusion.

Concern Analysis is such a reasoning process. It is a way of getting started, an untangling process, useful for isolating those parts of a generalised and complex situation which stand alone and on which different kinds of conclusions may be required. Sometimes Concern Analysis is unnecessary since the items requiring action are readily seen. Frequently however, situations are inherently complex and are not easy to separate. In these situations what often appears to happen is that over a period of time, a lot of different facets of the situation become interwoven and interrelated in the experience of the manager, until they appear as a large insoluble problem.

The reasoning processes of a manager cannot be realistically considered in isolation from the emotional aspects of his life. We have found frequently, that a manager who can handle the reasoning processes easily for someone else's job situation has difficulty in applying the same reasoning processes in his own situation, because of his emotional involvement.

In essence therefore, it is felt that a problem finding/concern identification process should not only assist in separating situations into discrete concerns - problem identification - but in;

.   identifying items for further action such as opportunities for improvement, or potential future threats.

.   setting priorities on those sub-parts in terms of their impact, time characteristics and growth potential.

.   Selecting the reasoning process necessary to develop the required conclusion for each separate concern.

.   Facilitating the manager's coping with the emotional component of his problems.

A.   Concern Analysis

Step 1.   Getting The Story

Purpose:

To enable the owner to talk out his situation and get clearer about its separate sub-parts and their inter-relationships.

To help the owner to recognise, accept and cope with his emotional stake in the situation.

To get a framework of "content" or background information, so that others working with the concern owner can generate useful process questions.

Procedure:
    Ask the concern owner to tell you about his problem. Allow him to ta
    freely and reinforce this by attention, acceptance, reflection of emotie
    ality, support and empathy. Allow him to run down.

    Avoid   evaluation,   diagnosis,   interruption   or   overt   processing
    information during this stage.

Step 2.   Questioning for Information

Purpose:
    To gain a perspective in which specific concerns can be teased ou
    identified and worked on separately.

    To reduce generality and fuziness by clarifying the identity, locatic
    timing and extent dimensions of the concern.

    To identify specific separate items on which further action may
    required.

Procedure:
    Ask open ended questions to elicit specific information or to clari
    information which has already been identified. For example,

    What are the strengths/weaknesses of the system?
    What goes right/wrong?

    Where in your department does .... affect you?
    Where in the process do you have trouble?

    When (time or date) does trouble occur?
    When else

    How much is it costing?
    How long has it been going on?

Step 3.   Listing Information

Purpose:
    To ensure, by making it visible and public, that the information used
    common to all parties.

    To get agreement on the accuracy of what each questioner has heard and
    which of these items requires further action.

    To pool and use the collective perceptions of all participants.

    To reinforce open information sharing.

Procedure:
    Each participant reads out "what he has learned" about the concern bei
    worked on and this is transcribed verbatim by one of the group (ideally
    flip charts).

    The concern owner verifies the accuracy of the data. The key task is
    list   the   information   quickly,   without   discussion   and   withou
    interpretation/evaluation by participants.

Step 4.   Identifying Items which require action

Purpose:

   .   To provide a list of discrete items on which action is required.

   .   To provide a basis for priority setting resource allocation, delegation, resource scheduling.

   .   To enable managers to work on one thing at a time, confident that they are working on the most important thing.

Procedure:

For each item ask:

Is this item a simple statement of fact? or is it an item that the concern owner needs to do something about?

Look out for:

   .   Potential problems; items on which present performance is meeting the standard but where improvement is possible.

   .   Opportunities; items where the actual performance achieved at an acceptable standard but is not reaching its full potential.

   .   Shortfalls; where actual performance is not reaching the required standard.

These three constitute three basic types of action items.

Step 5.   Review and Tighten

Purpose:

   .   To sharpen up the definition of action items.

   .   To eliminate duplications in the listing.

   .   To prevent over/under separation.

Procedure:

Each participant to read and examine the items identified as action items and to ask

   .   Is this item restating something which is said better elsewhere?

   .   Is each item stated clear unambiguus terms?

   .   What is meant by general terms eg. motivation?

eg: Ask what specifically are people not doing/doing that they should/ should not be doing.

   .   What labels are being applied to people?

eg: Poor attitude, lazy, apathetic.

In order to get an agreed listing ask.

What behaviours are being described here? What is that they do/do not do that tells you they are lazy etc.?

Step 6. Priority Setting

Purpose:

. To help the owner to feel that he has got to the heart of the matter; that the main issues have surfaced.

. To enable objective decisions to be made on.

- Which item to tackle first?

- How much time to allocate to each item on which action i required?

- What items should be delegated and to whom?

. To avoid setting priorities on the basis of which item is the mos fuss being made about.

Procedure:

Make visible information on each item under the three headings of serious ness, time availability and magnitude, especially where the priority i not obvious, where it is difficult to decide or where the task is bein shared and agreement is hard to reach.

Seriousness:

eg. Impact on responsibility, dollar cost, magnitude.

Ask and List:

What will happen if we don't deal with this?
Who else owns a piece of the action?

Time Availibility:

How much time do we have?
What would happen if we shelved it for "X" + 1, "X" + 2... etc days?

Magnitude:

How big was this concern in days past?
How big is it now?
How big will it be in future?

Step 7. Decide the next Process to Use

Purpose:

. In essence Concern Analysis is a problem identification process Having completed concern analysis, it is then necessary to get clea about what kind of further conclusion it is necessary to achieve fe each action item identified and then to select another reasoni process suitable for this task.

. To clarify the distinctive nature of the information needed in orde to read the required conclusion.

Procedure:

Ask: Is this an action item in which there is an unexpected a unexplained deviation between what should happen and what is actual happening?

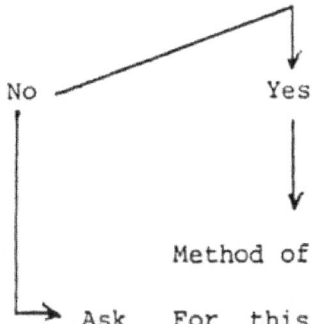

eg:

No   Yes

> A subordinates work has fallen off
> I don't know why and I need to know
> before I can fix it

Method of Analysis   =   Problem Analysis

Ask   For this action item do I have to choose the best of several possible alternatives from a range of ready made discrete alternatives to achieve an overall goal?

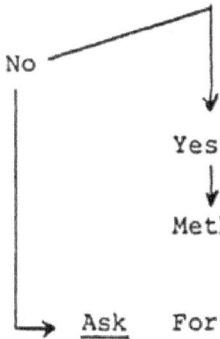

No

eg:

> Which brakes to fit to Trucks
> purchased in 1978

Yes

Method of Analysis   =   Decision Analysis

Ask   For this action item Do I have to develop a tailored "one off" solution to achieve an overall goal as no "pre-packaged" alternatives exist.

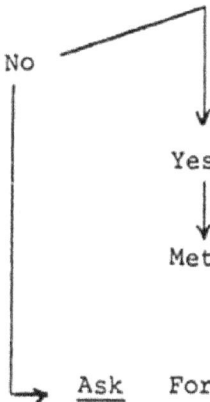

eg:

> What to do to improve operating
> efficiency of lubrication oil
> blending

No

Yes

Method of Analysis   =   Solution Development

Ask   For this action item am I concerned about what might go wrong in implementing a decision?

eg:

> To make sure new contracting
> procedures go according to plan

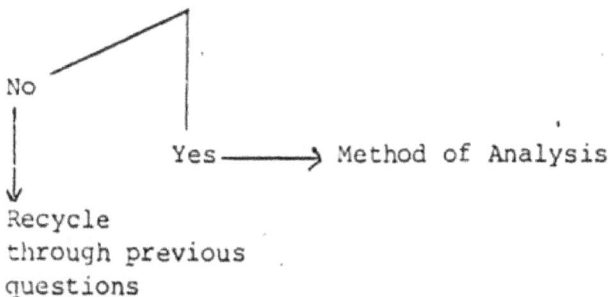

No

Yes ———> Method of Analysis   Potential Problem Analysis

Recycle
through previous
questions

B.   Decision Analysis (Choice between discrete alternatives)

In making a choice a manager is striving for balance between achieving t
most desirable effects possible, with the least undesirable effects, fr
a range of possible alternatives.   Initially, the decision maker needs
be clear about what decision is being made, which prior decisions a
assumed and at what level the decision is being made.   In this proce
judgement and experience play an important and integral part.

In order to achieve balance it is necessary to consider the impact
changes over time on alternatives which look like performing well in ter
of the results wanted and the intended resource utilisation.   In this w
a tentative choice, can be made with a significant degree of confiden
that it will hold up after implementation.

All of this, presupposes a range of alternatives can be generated fr
which to choose or is already available.   Additionally, in order to make
choice a standard of comparison, or more specifically, a picture of t
ideal outcomes or objectives is needed against which to compare.   Some
these outcomes will be essential and others desirable.   The desirab
objectives will vary according to their attractiveness and a system
weighting is used to determine their relative importance.

Decision Analysis

Step 1.   Decision Statement

Purpose:
   .   Defines the strategic goal to be achieved.

   .   Summarises prior decisions implicit in the decision now being made

   .   Defines the parameters of the choice being made in order to

          (a)   admit only relevant information.

          (b)   verify the decision is being made at the correct level.

          (c)   permit only valid objectives to be included.

Procedure:
   Ask   What would be a simple positive short label for this decision?

          Test to see if it tells you what the choice is about and and wk
          level it is being made.

          eg. Which Management Development Approach

          or

          What Course for Bloggs?

Step 2.   Establish Objectives

Purpose:
   .   To get clear about the results expected from the decision.

   .   To identify the resources available to aid or limit the decision.

   .   To assist in generating a range of alternatives from which
          choose.

. To make visible a composite picture of results and resources as criteria against which to compare and test alternatives.

. To focus the search for information about each alternative being considered.

Procedure:
Ask the owner of the decision, what results do you want from this decision?

Consider (superiors, subordinates, peers; competition, customers, trends, policy, law, R & D, past strengths and weakness).

What resource availability is relevant to your getting there?

Consider (space time authority, skill, manpower money, information and "know-how" equipment technology procedures).

What is it that you are trying to get out of this decision?

Step 3. Classify Objectives

Purpose:
Objectives may be thought of as either absolutely essential if the decision is to be effective (Musts) or desirable to some extent relative to each other. (Wants). By classifying objectives in this way the decision maker can

. Focus on what the decision must achieve.

. Eliminate from further consideration alternatives which do not meet the (Musts) essentional and uncompromisable standards of the (Musts).

. Narrow the range of alternatives to those which meet essential objectives (Musts).

. Flag for careful monitoring those alternatives which barely meet (Musts).

. Weight the (Want) Objectives in terms of their relative desirability for each decision.

. Decide in what order information about alternatives is to be processed.

It is possible that there are no (Must) objectives for a particular decision. However where they do exist, they should be tested throughly to make sure they are really Measurable, Practical and Realistic and Absolute.

Procedure:
Ask .   which limits are already imposed for this decision?
         eg. Coy. policy, Government legislation, Law.

     .   which of these are expressed in terms of a standard which is measurable and absolute?

Call these (Musts). The remaining objectives are (Wants).

To weight (Wants) a numeric scale with (10) given to the mc desirable want(s). All others are scored in relationship to the t one.

Compare alternatives by asking:

Which of these objectives is most important?
(10) weight

Compare the others in turn by asking:

Relative to how much I want .... (10 weight(s))
How much do I want .... this one

Review Objectives

To determine if they are clear, accurate and representative of a interests (balanced).

Procedure: Check to see if objectives are

. Accurate, refined, and in conformity with classifications.

. Omitted.

. A combination of objectives already stated separately.

. Duplicated.

. Representative of all valid interests.

. Valid results wanted/resources and not alternatives.

Step 4. Develop Alternatives

Purpose:
. To provide an acceptable basis for choice, in terms of both numb and variety, from a range of ready made„ new or modifications pre-existing alternatives.

. To narrow the range of alternatives to those which look l reasonable performers, relative to the overall goal set out in decision statement.

Procedure:
Use the objectives as a blueprint, to narrow down the total range possible alternatives, to those which merit detailed consideration in tl decision.

Ask: Does this alternative satisfy all essential objectives (Musts)?

If so, does it give me something of the most important result want?

Does the amount of resources it uses up, look reasonable?

Step 5.   Evaluate Alternatives against Objectives

Purpose:
-    To eliminate alternatives which do not meet the mandatory standards of the (Musts).

-    To display current and accurate information about each objective as a basis for objective evaluation of performance against (Musts).

-    To achieve a consistent comparable evaluation of the differing degree to which alternatives satisfy want objectives.

-    To make it possible to make public the processes and judgement inherent in the ultimate choice.

Procedure:
Make the most current and accurate information available visible by writing it in a work sheet, if working alone, or by displaying it on flip charts if working in a group.

Ask does this alternative meet the standards set for acceptance in the (Musts)?

Yes - consider it further.

No - eliminate it from further consideration. If all alternatives are rejected, then either other alternatives are needed or standards are too tight. Conversly, if all alternatives pass through the standards may be inappropriate or too loose.

For remaining alternatives, starting with the most important objective

-    Write in key-point information for each alternative under consideration relative to each want objective.

Ask   which alternative performs best against this objective?
Give it a score of (10)

which alternative is the next best performer .... for this one, how does it compare against our base score of 10?

Score accordingly.

Step 6.   Tentatively Choose the best Alternative.

Purpose:
-    To identify the one or two alternatives that are the best fit for this decision, when compared against the Want objectives.

-    To eliminate those alternatives which are the poorest performers.

Procedure:
Ask which alternative(s) considered give me the most results for the least in resources committed, as defined by the objectives for this decision.

Ask. If I select the best performing alternative will I be worse off than I am at present?

Step 7. Assess Adverse Consequences

Purpose:
.   To discover how well the alternative will hold up in the future.

.   To anticipate how an alternative will hold up in the light
     changing conditons.

.   To determine if crucial factors have been overlooked prior
     implementation.

Procedure:
     Give time and thought to each alternative as it might be in the futur
     forecasting what could go wrong with it.

     Do adverse consequences preculude the achievement of objectives?

Ask
.   What could go wrong, how could it hurt us?

     Write in the form of a statement which says what will go wrong a
     the undesirable effect this may have.
     eg. Costs will rise, inadequate return on investment.

.   Think about systems, people, methods materials, external influence
     money organisation, facilities and equipment.

.   Check out how surprise, newness, change, interfaces, skill
     reserves lead times, inflexibility etc. relative to the factors ir
     above.

.   Assign each consequence of vale of 10 - 1 in terms of i
     seriousness magnitude and impact e.g. (10 = disaster, 1 = mid
     uncomfortable).

.   Assign each serious consequence a value of 10 - 1 on the probabili
     of its occurrence (10 = certainty, 1 = 1 change in 10).

Step 8. Final Choice

Purpose:
     To double check completeness of objectives, appropriateness of standar
     on Musts, correctness of weighting on Wants, accuracy and timeliness
     information, values assigned to information and seriousness of adver
     consequences.

Procedure:
     Make your final choice based on best performance on Want objective
     satisfaction of must objectives, and minimum serious adverse consequence

     Aim to arrive at a choice which provides a favourable balance
     advantages and disadvantages.

D. Problem Analysis (to find the true cause of a deviation between actual performance and standard performance)

Problem analysis is a process which assists in a systematic way, with finding out the true cause of unexpected and unexplained trouble. It is a valuable management tool, since attempts to fix trouble without being clear on its true cause is at best, a hit and miss affair and at worst, is highly expensive and frustrating.

The two key concepts in Problem Analysis are:

(i)   that there is an unexpected and unexplained deviation between actual and standard performance which requires an explanation.

(ii) That this deviation is caused by change which is acting in, on or around a unique feature of the trouble area to cause the problem. It is in this way, that the problem acquires its unique identity, location, timing and magnitude.

On completion of a problem analysis a manager is aiming to have the most likely cause for the trouble he faces, so that he can take verifying action to prove that he has found the real cause with a reasonable chance that he will be successful.

In order to arrive at the most likely cause for the trouble; the manager should have considered a range of possible causes, including whatever hunches there are and have eliminated all the least likely ones, to end up with the cause which is most likely.

A range of possible causes can be developed by brainstorming but a more productive method is to focus on the differences and changes which exist in the trouble area, which do not exist in areas which are trouble free but where one might have expected to have had trouble.

In order to find these critical distinctions and through them the change or changes which have triggered the deviation; the problem is specified so that problem and non problem areas are bracketed in a precise picture of trouble. In this picture (Specification) the identity, timing, location and extent of both areas are described. Precise information is recorded under each of the four dimensions listed above for both the object which is defective and the defect itself.

This specification is both the basis for a focussed search for districtions and changes which are combined to generate possible causes for the problem. It also forms the basis for testing possible causes. These causes, must explain every aspect of both trouble and trouble free areas set out in the specification if they are not to be eliminated from consideration.

Step 1.   Deviation Statement

Purpose:
    To focus on the particular trouble under analysis by naming the specific
    deviation and its object.

    To confirm that there is a deviation between what performance should be
    and what it actually is.

    To provide a check on checks relevance of information under consideration.

Procedure:
    Identify the object affected and the nature of the deviation. Combine in
    a simple short statement which describes the item, group, process with
    which trouble has arisen and the nature of the trouble.

    Confirm that there is a difference between what performance actually is
    and what it should be.

Step 2.   Problem Specification

Purpose:
    To specifically define a problem's unique characteristics and boundary.
    (What it "is".)

    To define a similar but trouble free area which will sharply contrast with
    and delineate the trouble area. (What it "is not".)

    To act as basis for testing possible causes.

    To focus the search for unique features and changes which arise in or
    affect the trouble area.

    To identify which if any information is missing.

Procedure:
    In order to determine the boundaries of a particular problem we must
    define its unique characteristics by specifying that <u>identity</u> which sets
    it apart from things and conditions, its unique <u>location</u>, the specific
    <u>time</u> frame in which it occurs and that information which describes its
    particular <u>magnitude</u>.
    To do this we ask questions such as

             Trouble reported   Trouble reported
                  "is"   "is Not"

Identity
(What, Who)
    What "unit", "object", "process"   What closely associated "unit",
    "persons", is involved?   "process", "object", might be
                                         involved but is not"?

    specifically what is the trouble   What other trouble might we have
    with the object .... etc.?   expected but didn't get?

Location:

(Where)

Where geographically is the trouble observed.	Where geographically might the trouble have been observed but was not.
Where on the "object" does the trouble occur.	Where on the "object" might the trouble have occurred but didn't.

Timing:

(When)

When (clock or calendar time) was the trouble first observed.	At what other time might we have expected the trouble but didn't get it?
When in the life cycle of the "object" was the "defect" first observed.	At what other time in the life cycle of the "object", might trouble have been observed but it wasn't?

Magnitude

(How much
 trend)

How many defective "objects" are there.	How many defective "objects" might have but didn't occur?
How many "defects" per "object"	How many "defects" per object might have been expected but didn't arise.

In particular problems general terms like "object", "defect" which were shown above in quotation marks should be replaced with the normal names involved.

eg.   In Magnitude

How many "customer complaints" are there?

How many "complaints" might we have expected but didn't arise?

Step 3.   Develop Possible Causes

Purpose:
     To minimise the dependency on hunch and random speculation.

     To speed up the process of finding the true cause.

     To make public provisional statements about cause and effect, which can
     subsequentally tested.

     To eliminate irrelevant information, by developing   causes   thro
     distinctions of the trouble area and changes   in   or about th
     distinction.

Procedure:
     For   each of the four dimensions of the specification, (what, where w
     and extent) compare the information which defines what the problem '
     from what it "is not".

     Ask.   What is peculiar about "is" but different   about "is not"

What is true   about "is" which is in no way true   of "is not"?

          unique   unique
          different   different
          special   special

Distinctions are new information not already present in the specification w
set apart the trouble area "is" from the trouble free area "is not".

For each distinction ask

What has been improved
          changed
          altered   about this and when? (date all changes)
          stopped
          started
          etc.

Using combinations of the changes and distinctions which have been identif
construct provisional statements of cause and effect which assert how
change produced this problem Be specific.   Phrase all possible causes
positive testable language.

     Ask.   What is there about this change
                              plus a distinction   that could cause this
                              plus a change   deviation?

Step 4.   Test for most Probable Cause

Purpose:
     So that all hunches and changes and distinctions can be vetted to s
     they could cause the problem.

     To rigorously test each possible cause, so that all contradici
     assumptions, assertions, hedges and qualifications are identified, a
     and made visible.

     To increase confidence that the correct conclusion will be reache
     testing negatively, by shooting down, causes which don't explain al
     specification.

Procedure:
    Taking each cause, check out if it explains each entry in the "is", side
    of the specification and its corresponding entry on the "is not" side.

    Ask   If .... is the cause does it explain (read off "is") and why it
           "is not" (read off is not).

    Eliminate those which fail to explain both sides. Identify all
    assumptions in the most likely cause.

Step 5.   Verify for the True Cause

Purpose:
    To increase confidence that the cause found by logic is the real cause.

    To check out accuracy of information used in process.

    To ensure the most likely cause stands up in the real world.

    Managers are often "laymen" in terms of technology and often the technical
    details implicit in the most likely cause must be provided by someone with
    the necessary technical background.

Procedure:
    Search out further information about assumptions identified during testing
    of the most likely cause.

    Get further "on the scene" information by directly testing observing,
    discussing with those involved.

    Take action to see if the change implicit in the probable cause makes the
    problem go away.

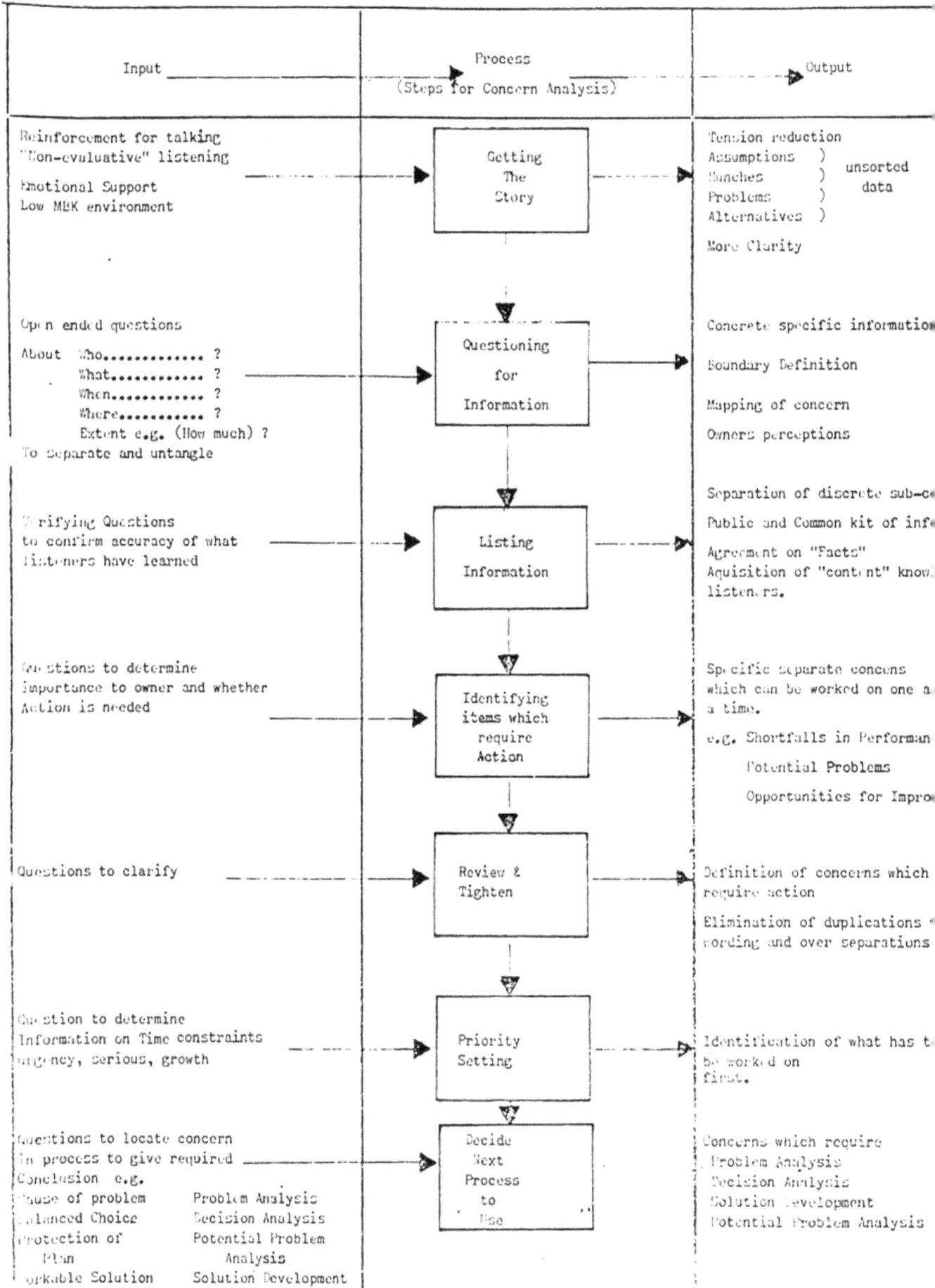

Input	Process (Steps for Concern Analysis)	Output
Reinforcement for talking "Non-evaluative" listening Emotional Support Low MBK environment	**Getting The Story**	Tension reduction Assumptions) Hunches) unsorted Problems) data Alternatives) More Clarity

Open ended questions
About Who............. ?
       What............ ?
       When............ ?
       Where........... ?
       Extent e.g. (How much) ?
To separate and untangle
	Questioning for Information	Concrete specific information
		
		Boundary Definition
		
		Mapping of concern
		
		Owners perceptions

Clarifying Questions to confirm accuracy of what listeners have learned	**Listing Information**	Separation of discrete sub-co Public and Common kit of inf Agreement on "Facts" Aquisition of "content" know listeners.

Questions to determine
importance to owner and whether
Action is needed
	Identifying items which require Action	Specific separate concerns
		which can be worked on one a
		a time.
		
		e.g. Shortfalls in Performan
		      Potential Problems
		      Opportunities for Impro

Questions to clarify	**Review & Tighten**	Definition of concerns which require action Elimination of duplications wording and over separations
Question to determine Information on Time constraints urgency, serious, growth	**Priority Setting**	Identification of what has t be worked on first.
Questions to locate concern in process to give required Conclusion e.g. Cause of problem Problem Analysis Balanced Choice Decision Analysis Protection of Potential Problem Plan Analysis Workable Solution Solution Development	**Decide Next Process to Use**	Concerns which require Problem Analysis Decision Analysis Solution Development Potential Problem Analysis

Problem Solving: (Problem Analysis to find the True Cause of a   60
deviation between actual performance and Standard
Performance)

Input	Process (Steps in Problem Analysis)	Output
•Information about identity of trouble and object, place person, group affected. Comparision between actual performance and standard performance.	Deviation Statement	Name of "object" affected and nature of "defect, or "deviation".
•Information which defines characteristics of the deviation in terms of its identity location timing and extent and information. Contrasting the problem with a trouble free area where trouble might have been expected to occur but did not.	Problem Specification	A clear boundary line round the problem. A basis for finding distinctions and developing possible causes. Specific information against which to test possible causes.
•Information about quality features or characteristics of the problem which are not true of the problem free area (distinctions). •Information about changes which have occurred in or around or on these distinctions	Develop Possible Causes	Specific statements of possible causes for the particular problem specified.
In respect of each cause, questions which try to elicit information which will bring about the failure of the 'possible cause" to explain each side of specification on each dimension to (identify, location, timing and extent)	Test for Most Probable Cause	The Most Probable Cause or The most probable cause plus assumptions necessary to support it.
Further information to check out any implicit assumptions or Further information from direct on site observation or Information about trials to verify results.	Verify for the True Cause	True Cause or Problem (Deviation)

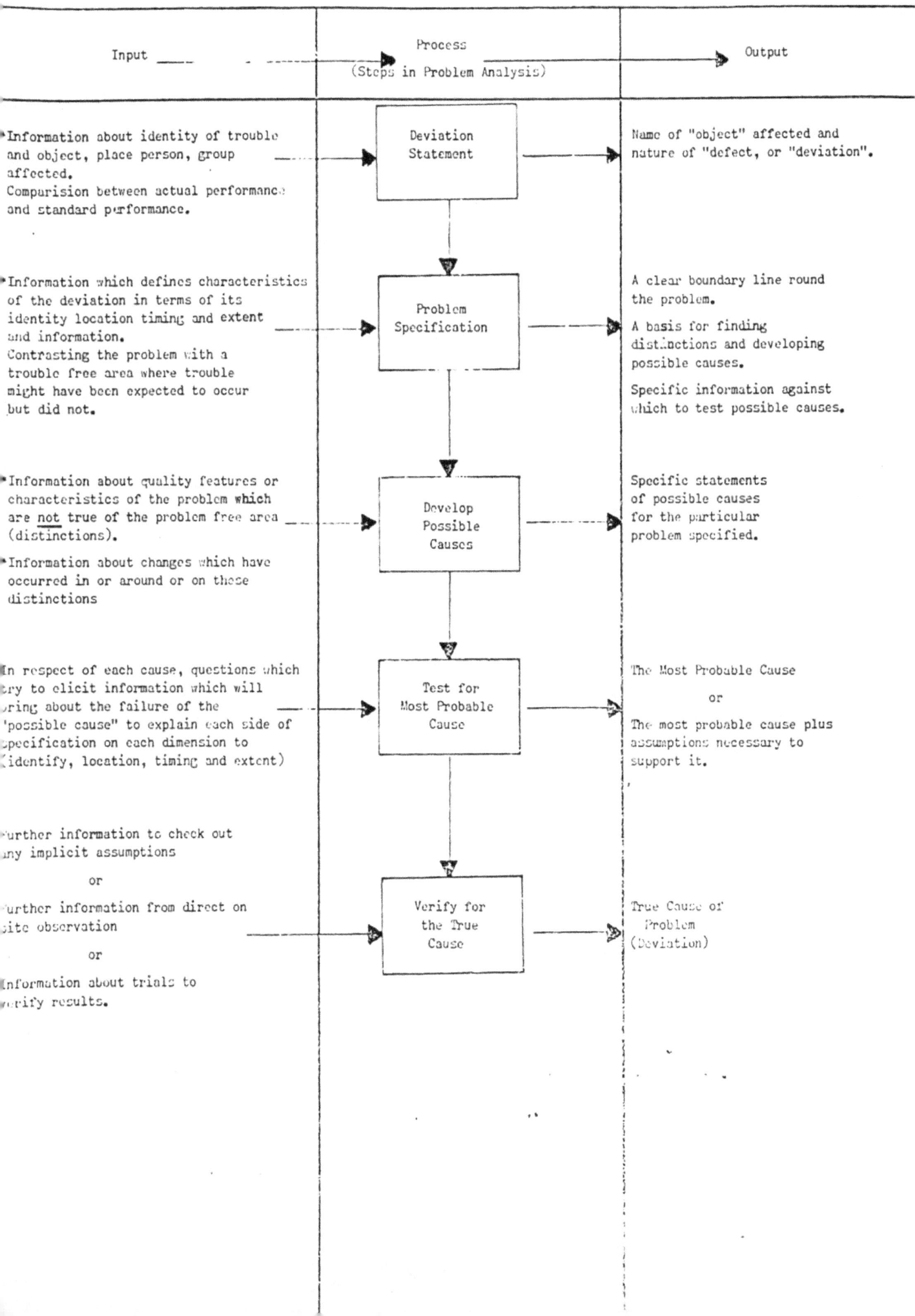

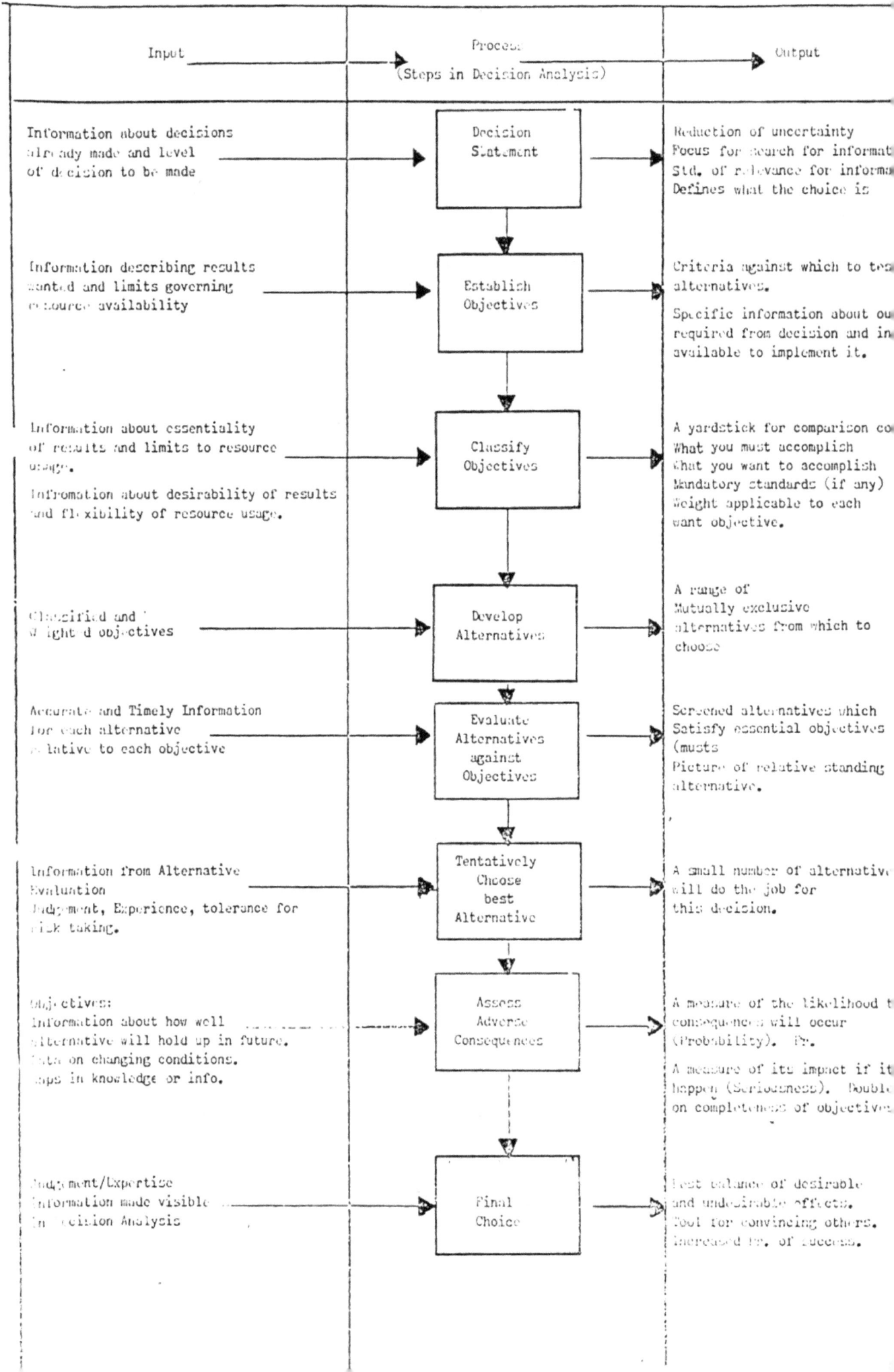

Decision making (Choice between discrete alternatives)

Input	Process (Steps in Decision Analysis)	Output
Information about decisions already made and level of decision to be made	**Decision Statement**	Reduction of uncertainty Focus for search for informati Std. of relevance for informa Defines what the choice is
Information describing results wanted and limits governing resource availability	**Establish Objectives**	Criteria against which to te alternatives. Specific information about ou required from decision and in available to implement it.
Information about essentiality of results and limits to resource usage. Information about desirability of results and flexibility of resource usage.	**Classify Objectives**	A yardstick for comparison co What you must accomplish What you want to accomplish Mandatory standards (if any) Weight applicable to each want objective.
Classified and weighted objectives	**Develop Alternatives**	A range of Mutually exclusive alternatives from which to choose
Accurate and Timely Information for each alternative relative to each objective	**Evaluate Alternatives against Objectives**	Screened alternatives which Satisfy essential objectives (musts Picture of relative standing alternative.
Information from Alternative Evaluation Judgment, Experience, tolerance for risk taking.	**Tentatively Choose best Alternative**	A small number of alternative will do the job for this decision.
Objectives: Information about how well alternative will hold up in future. Data on changing conditions. Gaps in knowledge or info.	**Assess Adverse Consequences**	A measure of the likelihood t consequences will occur (Probability). Pr. A measure of its impact if it happen (Seriousness). Double on completeness of objectives
Judgment/Expertise Information made visible in Decision Analysis	**Final Choice**	Best balance of desirable and undesirable effects. Tool for convincing others. Increased Pr. of success.

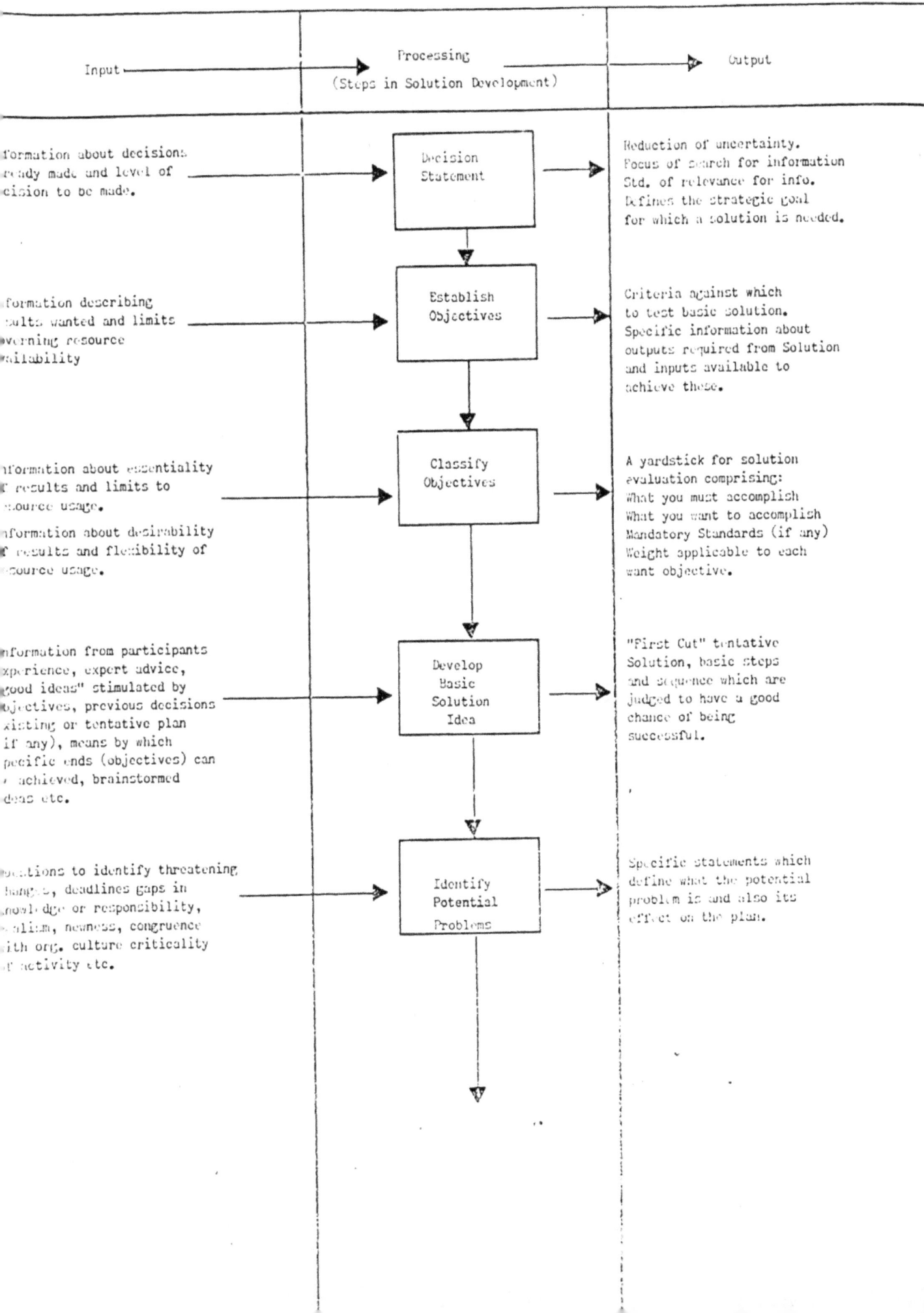

Decision Making: (Tailoring a solution to satisfy an overall goal   62
where no range of ready made discrete alternatives
exists)

Input	Processing (Steps in Solution Development)	Output
Information about decisions already made and level of decision to be made.	**Decision Statement**	Reduction of uncertainty. Focus of search for information Std. of relevance for info. Defines the strategic goal for which a solution is needed.
Information describing results wanted and limits governing resource availability	**Establish Objectives**	Criteria against which to test basic solution. Specific information about outputs required from Solution and inputs available to achieve these.
Information about essentiality of results and limits to resource usage. Information about desirability of results and flexibility of resource usage.	**Classify Objectives**	A yardstick for solution evaluation comprising: What you must accomplish What you want to accomplish Mandatory Standards (if any) Weight applicable to each want objective.
Information from participants experience, expert advice, "good ideas" stimulated by objectives, previous decisions existing or tentative plan (if any), means by which specific ends (objectives) can be achieved, brainstormed ideas etc.	**Develop Basic Solution Idea**	"First Cut" tentative Solution, basic steps and sequence which are judged to have a good chance of being successful.
Questions to identify threatening changes, deadlines gaps in knowledge or responsibility, realism, newness, congruence with org. culture criticality of activity etc.	**Identify Potential Problems**	Specific statements which define what the potential problem is and also its effect on the plan.

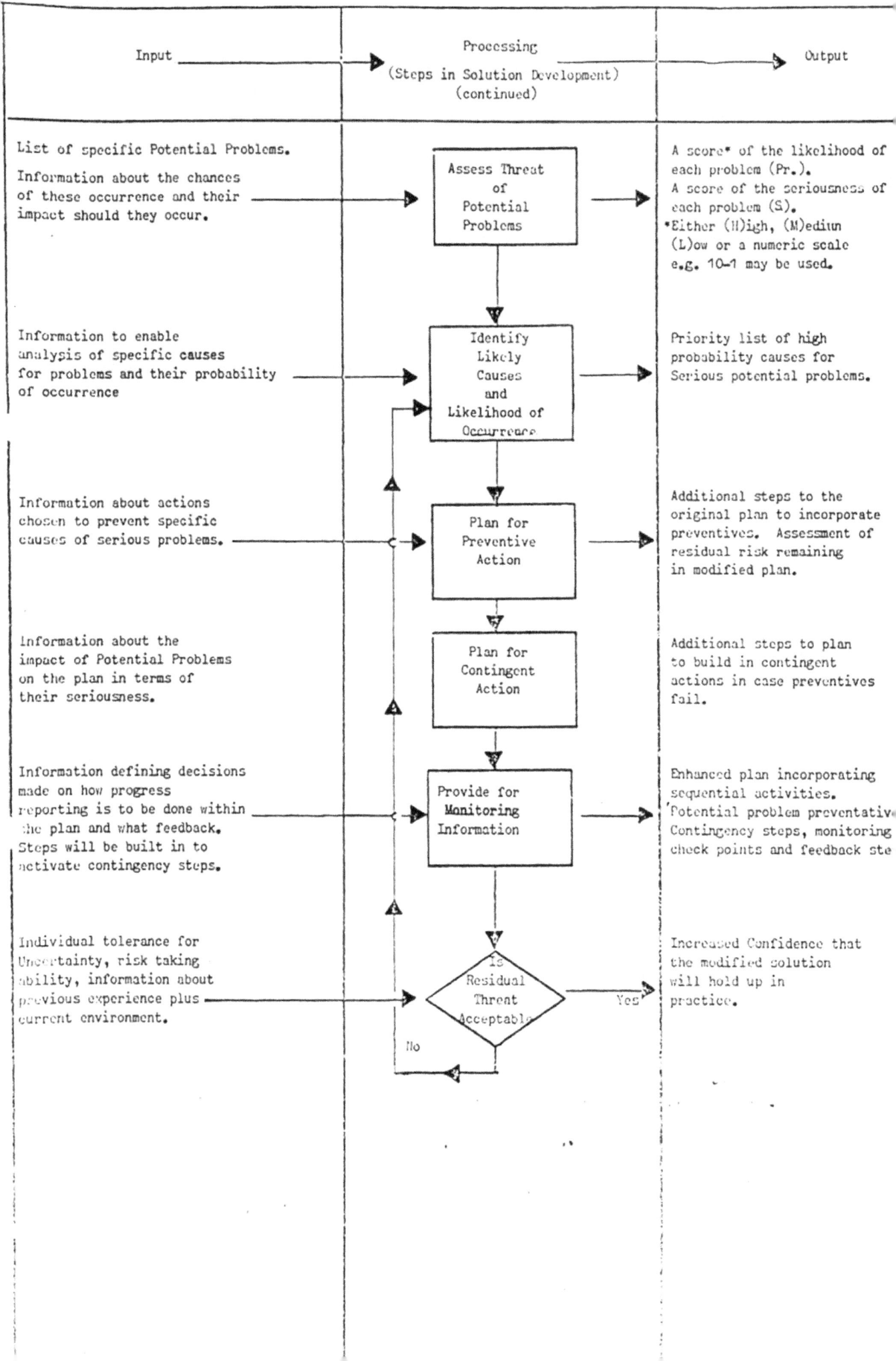

Input	Processing (Steps in Solution Development) (continued)	Output

List of specific Potential Problems.

Information about the chances of these occurrence and their impact should they occur.

Assess Threat of Potential Problems

A score* of the likelihood of each problem (Pr.).
A score of the seriousness of each problem (S).
*Either (H)igh, (M)edium (L)ow or a numeric scale e.g. 10-1 may be used.

Information to enable analysis of specific causes for problems and their probability of occurrence

Identify Likely Causes and Likelihood of Occurrence

Priority list of high probability causes for Serious potential problems.

Information about actions chosen to prevent specific causes of serious problems.

Plan for Preventive Action

Additional steps to the original plan to incorporate preventives. Assessment of residual risk remaining in modified plan.

Information about the impact of Potential Problems on the plan in terms of their seriousness.

Plan for Contingent Action

Additional steps to plan to build in contingent actions in case preventives fail.

Information defining decisions made on how progress reporting is to be done within the plan and what feedback. Steps will be built in to activate contingency steps.

Provide for Monitoring Information

Enhanced plan incorporating sequential activities. Potential problem preventative Contingency steps, monitoring check points and feedback ste

---

Individual tolerance for Uncertainty, risk taking ability, information about previous experience plus current environment.

Is Residual Threat Acceptable

No

Yes

Increased Confidence that the modified solution will hold up in practice.

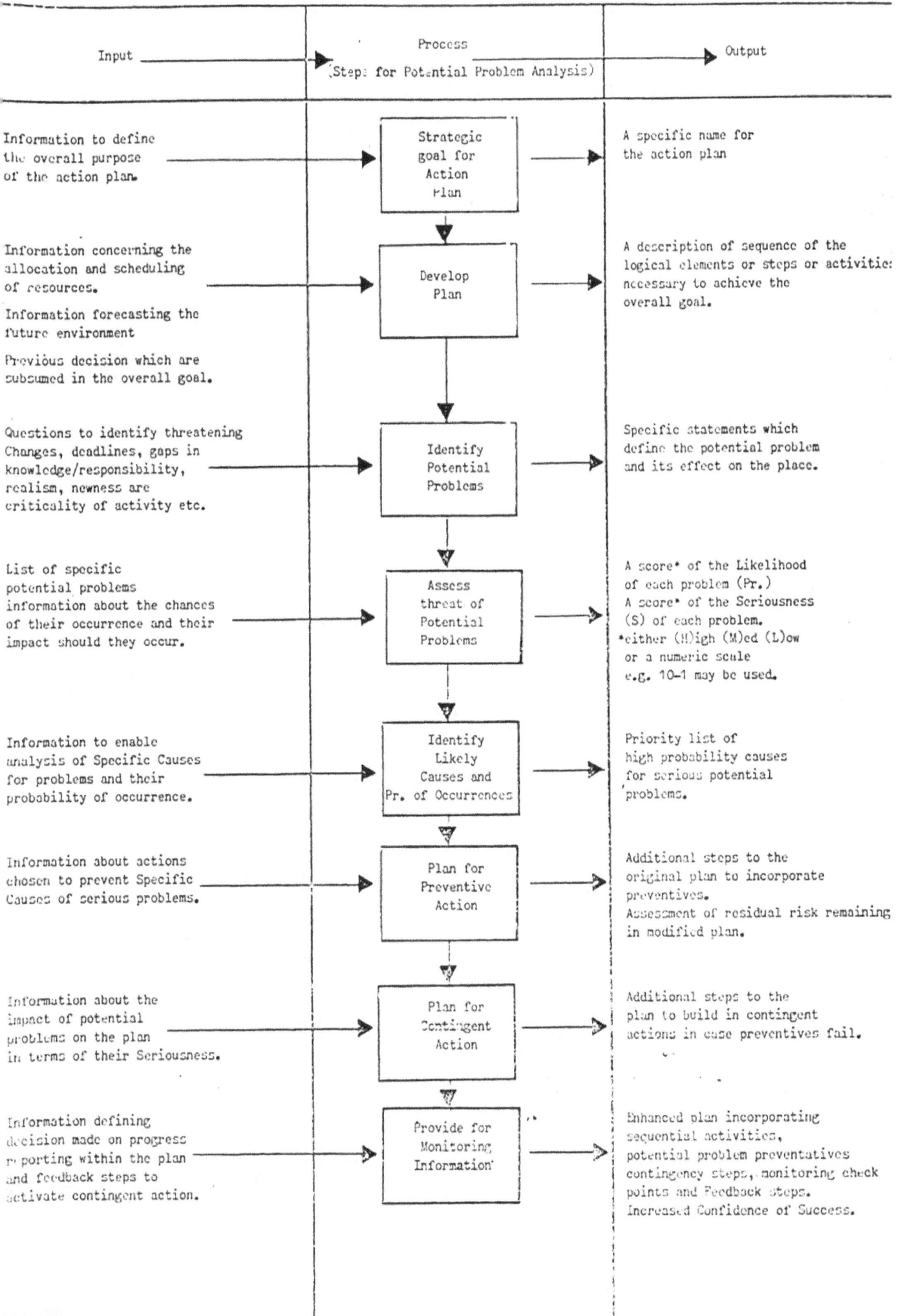

Input	Process (Steps for Potential Problem Analysis)	Output
Information to define the overall purpose of the action plan.	Strategic goal for Action Plan	A specific name for the action plan
Information concerning the allocation and scheduling of resources. Information forecasting the future environment. Previous decision which are subsumed in the overall goal.	Develop Plan	A description of sequence of the logical elements or steps or activities necessary to achieve the overall goal.
Questions to identify threatening Changes, deadlines, gaps in knowledge/responsibility, realism, newness are criticality of activity etc.	Identify Potential Problems	Specific statements which define the potential problem and its effect on the place.
List of specific potential problems information about the chances of their occurrence and their impact should they occur.	Assess threat of Potential Problems	A score* of the Likelihood of each problem (Pr.) A score* of the Seriousness (S) of each problem. *either (H)igh (M)ed (L)ow or a numeric scale e.g. 10-1 may be used.
Information to enable analysis of Specific Causes for problems and their probability of occurrence.	Identify Likely Causes and Pr. of Occurrences	Priority list of high probability causes for serious potential problems.
Information about actions chosen to prevent Specific Causes of serious problems.	Plan for Preventive Action	Additional steps to the original plan to incorporate preventives. Assessment of residual risk remaining in modified plan.
Information about the impact of potential problems on the plan in terms of their Seriousness.	Plan for Contingent Action	Additional steps to the plan to build in contingent actions in case preventives fail.
Information defining decision made on progress reporting within the plan and feedback steps to activate contingent action.	Provide for Monitoring Information	Enhanced plan incorporating sequential activities, potential problem preventatives contingency steps, monitoring check points and Feedback steps. Increased Confidence of Success.

A Systems Model depicting the relationship between an Organisation and Management Processes

Organisational
Variables

Problem Solving and Decision
making Processes.

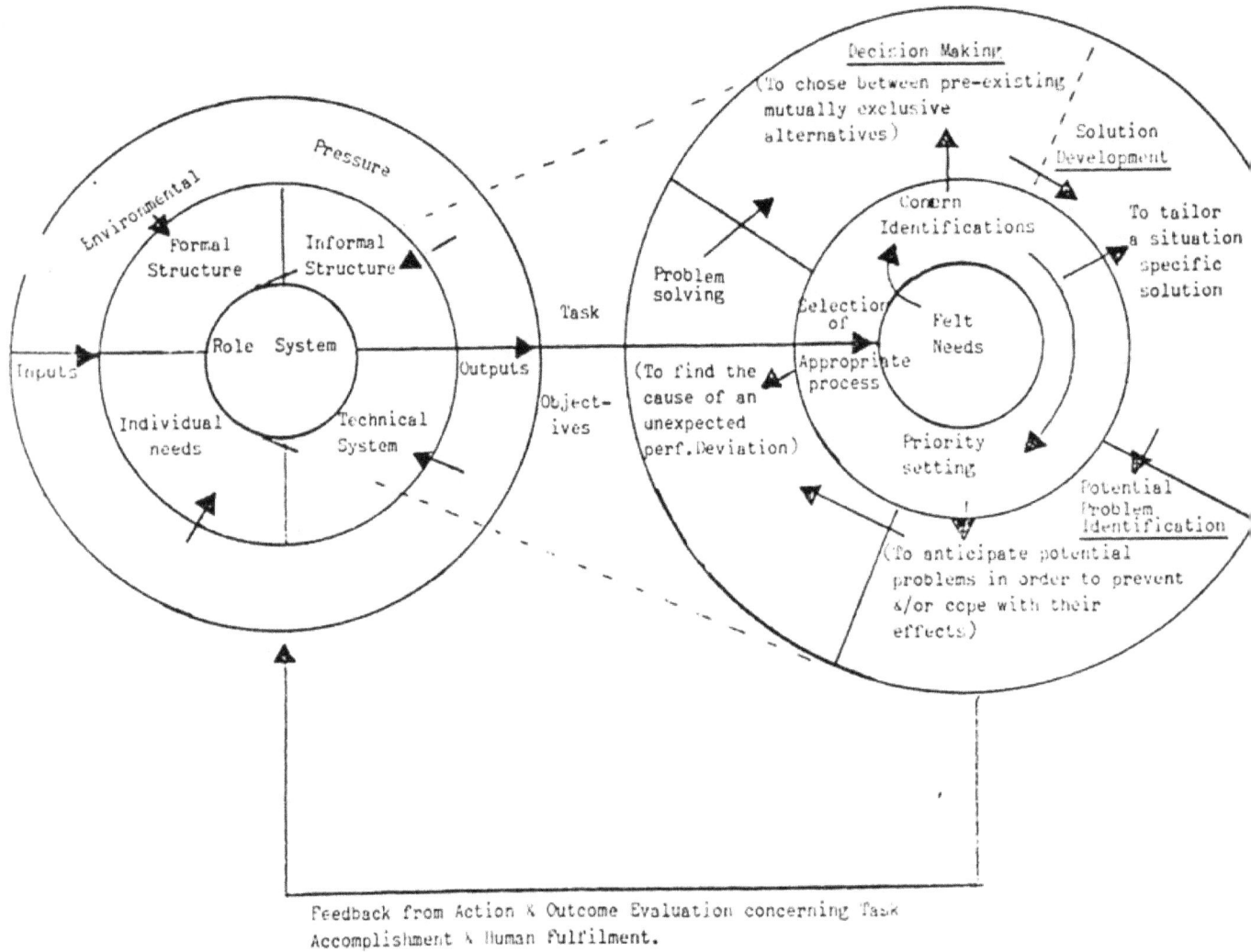

Decision Making
(To chose between pre-existing
mutually exclusive
alternatives)

Solution
Development

Environmental

Pressure

Formal
Structure

Informal
Structure

To tailor
a situation
specific
solution

Concern
Identifications

Problem
solving

Task

Role   System

Felt
Needs

Selection
of
Appropriate
process

Inputs

Outputs

Objectives

(To find the
cause of an
unexpected
perf.Deviation)

Individual
needs

Technical
System

Priority
setting

Potential
Problem
Identification

(To anticipate potential
problems in order to prevent
&/or cope with their
effects)

Feedback from Action & Outcome Evaluation concerning Task
Accomplishment & Human Fulfilment.

APPENDIX B

Synopsis of Responses to Question 7

<u>Shell</u>   <u>Trained</u>

(1)   Good lecturer in a seminary - taught me logic.

(2)   Working on my own in auditing. I had a
       good manager.

(3)   My first job as a supervisor.

(4)   Mixing with people who were good. Working
       under pressure for a superb manager.

(5)   Going into a job I had never tackled before.
       2 good managers in particular.

(6)   My first 3 years as a manager: I worked
       for a brilliant man.

(7)   Regular army officer. Staff captain to a
       Brigadier. He was terrific.

(8)   Being posted to Darwin, P.N.G. isolated
       from others, thrown on my own resources.

<u>Untrained</u>

(1)   Crusty professional manager, he would punch
       holes, expected me to learn quickly. He
       was hard. But scrupulously fair.

(2)   Being promoted to first supervisor job.
       I had a good general manager. I could talk
       to him. He was fair, he encouraged well
       considered risks.

Appendix B - continued

(3)   Writing publishable material one has to be
        very critical. A particularly demanding
        professor. I was bored with being an academic
        so I joined Shell.

(4)   A terrific bloke I worked for, he was
        very impressive, I will never forget him.
        It was always an education to listen to
        him. Clear accountability is what counts.

(5)   Times when I have been forced to make a
        decision. Death of father. Chose to do
        M.B.A.

(6)   Navy training. Special school teacher.

(7)   A manager I worked for was a man of
        vision, he made things clear for me. He
        made me think in more depth.

Australia Post Trained

(1)   A good manager I had for three years.

(2)   Working in a very demanding job straight
        from University. I had a terrific
        manager.

(3)   Lost everything in bushfire, came to
        Melbourne. I was alone, had to learn by
        doing. Had an excellent manager.

(4)   I had a fatherly manager.

(5)   I sought out a demanding position. I saw
       more of the world as it really is. The
       manager taught me how to think. I had
       something to build on after that.

(6)   Doing logic at tertiary level. Self
       confidence is only built by taking
       responsibility for oneself.

(7)   My dad taught me diagnostics, to be
       critical. He was anti academic.

(8)   In Brisbane I had a boss who had great
       faith in me. He really showed me what I
       was made of.

(9)   Working for a manager who could define
       goals.

(10)   A real human being who lived life to the
       full. He turned me on, I owe him a lot.

(11)   My training as an engineer. I had
       responsibility very early in life. I had
       to work things out for myself.

(12)   Working with a dedicated man. He gave
       himself to developing others.

(13)   Worked for a fantastic team leader.

(14)   Great manager I work for now, he is the best.

(15)   My academic studies in past 5 years.

(16)   My time as an inspector working for an especially competent manager.

(17)   I worked for a hatchet man, he kept his personal life separate from business, he really influenced me.

Untrained

(1)   My continuing study, with stimulating people.

(2)   When I first took responsibility for myself. I had a complex job and a great boss.

(3)   I worked for a really analytic man for 3 years. He taught me how to deal with complexity.

(4)   My first management job really gave me the feedback I needed. I had a manager who was highly moral and upright. He was great.

(5)   I had a manager whose judgment was excellent, he taught me a lot.

Appendix B   -   continued

(6)   Working for people who demanded high
       standards. I left home at 13, people are
       too dependent these days.

(7)   Experience in a number of jobs, I'm stale
       now I've been here 3 years. My
       manager backs me up though.

(8)   Between '67-'75 when I moved into middle
       management I had a particularly good sponsor.
       He really coached me.

(9)   A role model: a man I worked for about
       7 years ago. He was thoughtful and a good
       tutor. He made me think.

(10)   I'm turned on now, my manager's great.

(11)   I entered uni early, had an influential
       friend, he was older & intellectually
       powerful.

(12)   When I was in P.N.G. I was 35-39. I had
       a superb mentor.

(13)   Any time I have had a challenge I have
       developed a bit more.

(14)   Boy scout leader, mum was more decisive than
       dad and I picked that up.

(15)   One man I worked for, for 3 years.

Appendix B   -   continued

(16)   My post graduate degree taught me to think
        independently. A particular man taught me
        how to cope with ambiguity.

(17)   I worked for a man who taught me how to sort
        out the important issues from the unimportant.

(18)   The examples given by others. One of my
        parents was hopeless. I worked for a good
        manager early in my career and that made
        up for the poor parenting.

(19)   Only way of learning is by experimenting &
        using the feedback. 2 people have influenced
        me a lot. They were good developers. One was
        outstanding.

* * * * * * * R E L I A B I L I T Y   A N A L Y S I S   F O R   S C A L E   (O P S   ) * * * * * * * * *

CORRELATION MATRIX

	Q41	Q42	Q43	Q44	Q45	Q46	Q47	Q48	Q49	Q50
Q50	.18004	.23785	.33593	.27690	.41713	.17894	.54325	.40119	.23094	1.00000
Q51	.53905	.37041	.20607	.30202	-.00092	.41261	.41683	.29302	.25379	.29672
Q52	.48045	.52725	.43409	.20570	.09712	.69567	.29048	.52752	.30910	.31247
Q53	.44719	.24655	.22227	.33289	-.01084	.32982	.38512	.30483	.16673	.17329
Q54	.42181	.51881	.40566	.50719	.14606	.56591	.28196	.39642	.42325	.23978
Q55	.25827	.13750	.14444	.50172	.18662	.26617	.32196	.19527	.31168	.24926
Q56	.26563	.15852	.16153	.27407	.19133	.30385	.19884	.07894	.32929	.15631
Q57	.42486	.37723	.27912	.49044	.02606	.44175	.51632	.31046	.24062	.39451

CORRELATION MATRIX

	Q51	Q52	Q53	Q54	Q55	Q56	Q57
Q51	1.00000						
Q52	.40237	1.00000					
Q53	.47306	.36311	1.00000				
Q54	.42614	.62762	.40959	1.00000			
Q55	.35401	.26784	.39873	.44882	1.00000		
Q56	-.00250	.23333	.14036	.39807	.14895	1.00000	
Q57	.47085	.52435	.46147	.63967	.40092	.31488	1.00000

WARNING...DETERMINANT OF MATRIX IS 0.0. STATISTICS
BASED ON INVERSE OF MATRIX FOR SCALE OPS   CANNOT BE COMPUTED.

N OF CASES =   54.0

STATISTICS FOR   MEAN   VARIANCE   STD DEV   VARIABLES
     SCALE   202.81481   1075.62544   32.79673   57

	MEAN	MINIMUM	MAXIMUM	RANGE	MAX/MIN	VARIANCE
ITEM MEANS	3.55815	1.94444	4.53704	2.59259	2.33333	.28821
ITEM VARIANCES	.95053	.12893	2.19462	2.06569	17.02168	.10530

	MEAN	MINIMUM	MAXIMUM	RANGE	MAX/MIN	VARIANCE
INTER-ITEM COVARIANCES	.32000	-.15094	.81971	.97065	-5.43056	.01737
INTER-ITEM CORRELATIONS	.36369	-.12435	.74077	.86512	-5.95710	.02293

* * * * * R E L I A B I L I T Y   A N A L Y S I S   F O R   S C A L E   (O P 5   )   * * * * * * * * * *

ITEM-TOTAL STATISTICS

	SCALE MEAN IF ITEM DELETED	SCALE VARIANCE IF ITEM DELETED	CORRECTED ITEM-TOTAL CORRELATION	SQUARED MULTIPLE CORRELATION	ALPHA IF ITEM DELETED
01	199.07407	1035.08875	.76979	99.00000	.96552
02	199.16667	1037.68868	.64514	99.00000	.96580
03	198.88889	1035.57233	.74547	99.00000	.96557
04	199.79630	1046.80678	.37274	99.00000	.96675
05	198.38889	1033.63836	.72687	99.00000	.96558
06	198.98148	1040.13173	.67981	99.00000	.96576
07	198.38889	1037.56289	.69218	99.00000	.96570
08	200.46296	1045.95143	.28678	99.00000	.96758
09	199.70370	1040.28791	.62254	99.00000	.96588
010	198.79630	1037.78791	.78270	99.00000	.96556
011	200.00000	1046.45283	.36294	99.00000	.96683
012	199.42593	1047.20755	.36970	99.00000	.96675
013	199.42593	1040.73969	.53691	99.00000	.96611
014	199.00000	1041.66038	.66355	99.00000	.96582
015	198.77778	1030.96855	.68714	99.00000	.96564
016	199.79630	1035.97659	.62576	99.00000	.96584
017	199.03704	1033.96087	.71989	99.00000	.96560
018	199.09259	1034.61391	.55921	99.00000	.96607
019	198.92593	1038.97554	.57430	99.00000	.96600
020	198.85185	1047.18519	.41191	99.00000	.96653
021	198.27778	1034.31761	.73119	99.00000	.96558
022	199.94444	1049.52516	.43826	99.00000	.96639
023	198.92593	1027.91894	.71220	99.00000	.96555
024	199.14815	1035.22292	.53670	99.00000	.96616
025	198.88889	1040.70440	.61192	99.00000	.96591
026	199.37037	1028.72816	.65175	99.00000	.96574
027	198.42593	1028.77743	.81833	99.00000	.96532
028	199.33333	1029.43396	.57651	99.00000	.96604
029	199.14815	1034.01537	.66507	99.00000	.96559
030	199.83333	1037.57547	.59946	99.00000	.96572
031	198.87037	1028.45458	.75121	99.00000	.96592
032	198.92593	1038.90007	.75424	99.00000	.96545
033	199.50000	1039.39623	.70936	99.00000	.96562
034	199.55259	1035.30259	.50231	99.00000	.96624
035	199.09259	1036.23655	.74207	99.00000	.96559
036	199.57407	1050.96611	.29088	99.00000	.96715
037	198.83333	1039.34906	.55844	99.00000	.96605
038	199.50000	1043.72642	.60727	99.00000	.96595
039	199.55259	1056.81936	.32711	99.00000	.96668
040	199.75926	1040.51572	.64314	99.00000	.96569
041	199.09259	1039.95283	.61019	99.00000	.96591
042	200.14815	1044.01537	.53571	99.00000	.96612
043	199.33333	1038.18868	.48221	99.00000	.96637
044	199.50000	1039.04717	.53782	99.00000	.96612
045	200.46296	1056.81936	.32711	99.00000	.96668
046	198.83333	1027.87736	.66610	99.00000	.96569
047	200.87037	1060.75646	.63021	99.00000	.96630
048	198.81481	1033.51223	.55205	99.00000	.96611
049	198.66667	1039.05660	.55274	99.00000	.96607
050	198.81481	1042.22921	.46965	99.00000	.96636
051	199.44444	1039.00629	.61973	99.00000	.96587
052	199.03704	1032.52690	.68009	99.00000	.96567

053	199.31481	1039.50280	.53156	99.00000	.96614
054	198.96296	1025.43256	.74078	99.00000	.96545
055	199.50259	1042.32145	.54337	99.00000	.96609
056	199.90741	1047.29315	.33150	99.00000	.96702
057	198.87037	1037.39797	.64616	99.00000	.96580

A VALUE OF 99.0 IS PRINTED IF A COEFFICIENT CANNOT BE COMPUTED

RELIABILITY 1

FILE   NONAME   (CREATION DATE = 13/08/82)

13/08/82   16.02.27.   PAGE   19

* * * * * * R E L I A B I L I T Y   A N A L Y S I S   F O R   S C A L E   (O P S   ) * * * * * * * * *

ANALYSIS OF VARIANCE

SOURCE OF VARIATION	SS	DF	MEAN SQUARE	F	SIG.
BETWEEN PEOPLE	1000.14295	53	18.87062		
WITHIN PEOPLE	2742.94737	3024	.90706		
BETWEEN MEASURES	871.53476	56	15.56312	24.68261	.0001
RESIDUAL	1871.41261	2968	.63053		
NONADDITIVITY	13.78052	1	13.78052	22.01018	.0001
BALANCE	1857.63208	2967	.62610		
TOTAL	3743.09032	3077	1.21647		

GRAND MEAN =   3.55815

TUKEY ESTIMATE OF POWER TO WHICH OBSERVATIONS
MUST BE RAISED TO ACHIEVE ADDITIVITY =   .2150923

HOTELLINGS T-SQUARED CANNOT BE COMPUTED FOR SCALE OPS

RELIABILITY COEFFICIENTS   57 ITEMS

ALPHA = .96659   STANDARDIZED ITEM ALPHA =   .97022

APPENDIX C

APPENDIX

Means of Questionnaire items:

trained and untrained subjects

	TRAINED	UNTRAINED
Q1	3.74	3.41
Q2	3.78	3.5
Q3	3.93	3.93
Q4	3.11	2.93
Q5	4.52	4.33
Q6	3.89	3.77
Q7	4.44	4.4
Q8	2.48	2.22
Q9	3.19*	3.04
Q10	4.15	3.89
Q11	2.78*	2.85
Q12	4.00	3.63
Q13	3.56	3.22
Q14	4.04	3.59
Q15	4.11	3.96
Q16	3.19	2.85
Q17	4.04	3.52
Q18	3.82	3.65
Q19	4.00	3.78
Q20	4.07	3.89
Q21	4.67	4.41
Q22	2.93	2.82

Appendix   - continued

	TRAINED	UNTRAINED
Q23	4.07	3.70
Q24	3.85	3.48
Q25	4.00	3.85
Q26	3.67	3.22
Q27	4.63	4.15
Q28	3.67	3.29
Q29	3.70	3.63
Q30	3.15	2.81
Q31	4.19	3.70
Q32	4.04	3.74
Q33	3.85	3.78
Q34	3.30	3.22
Q35	3.82	3.63
Q36	3.41	3.07
Q37	4.11	3.85
Q38	3.33	3.29
Q39	3.37	3.07
Q40	3.11	3.00
Q41	3.44	3.18
Q42	2.85	2.48
Q43	3.70	3.26
Q44	3.48	3.15
Q45	2.59	2.11
Q46	4.11	3.85

Appendix   - continued

	TRAINED	UNTRAINED
Q47	1.93*	1.96
Q48	4.04	3.96
Q49	4.41	3.89
Q50	4.19	3.82
Q51	3.37*	3.37
Q52	4.04	3.52
Q53	3.26*	3.74
Q54	4.11	3.59
Q55	3.48	2.96
Q56	3.04	2.78
Q57	4.00	3.89

Significant Spearman Rank Correlations

Level of education	Information Processing Style 5 + .28 (Narrow range of options) p<.05 Jumping to conclusions
Sex	Anticipatory Regret Info.Proc. Style 3 + .36 p<.005 Females report more conflict & inertia when facing important decisions
Sex	Post decisional Regret Info.Processing Style 2 - .36 p<.005 Females report less Post Decisional Regret
Age	Factor 4 (Active Independence) + .36 p<.005 Older people score more highly on Factor 4.
Age	Factor 2 (organised information) + .24 p<.05 Older people organise decision making information.
Sex	Factor 4 (Active Independence) - .30 p<.05 Females score less highly on active independence.

3, 1

PRINCIPAL COMPONENTS 1

FILE NONAME (CREATION DATE = 16/08/82)

16/08/82   15:07:55.   PAGE   4

VARIABLE	EST COMMUNALITY	FACTOR	EIGENVALUE	PCT OF VAR	CUM PCT
Q1	1.00000	1	22.32938	39.2	39.2
Q2	1.00000	2	3.49196	6.1	45.3
Q3	1.00000	3	2.61893	4.6	49.9
Q4	1.00000	4	2.39032	4.2	54.1
Q5	1.00000	5	2.03897	3.6	57.7
Q6	1.00000	6	1.95762	3.4	61.1
Q7	1.00000	7	1.71003	3.0	64.1
Q8	1.00000	8	1.59287	2.8	66.9
Q9	1.00000	9	1.50979	2.6	69.5
Q10	1.00000	10	1.30916	2.3	71.8
Q11	1.00000	11	1.28772	2.3	74.1
Q12	1.00000	12	1.26943	2.2	76.3
Q13	1.00000	13	1.09221	1.9	78.2
Q14	1.00000	14	.94884	1.7	79.9
Q15	1.00000	15	.91990	1.6	81.5
Q16	1.00000	16	.86830	1.5	83.0
Q17	1.00000	17	.79470	1.4	84.4
Q18	1.00000	18	.77428	1.4	85.8
Q19	1.00000	19	.70673	1.2	87.0
Q20	1.00000	20	.65519	1.1	88.2
Q21	1.00000	21	.61512	1.1	89.3
Q22	1.00000	22	.57963	1.0	90.3
Q23	1.00000	23	.51168	.9	91.2
Q24	1.00000	24	.49503	.9	92.0
Q25	1.00000	25	.43569	.8	92.8
Q26	1.00000	26	.41321	.7	93.5
Q27	1.00000	27	.37336	.7	94.2
Q28	1.00000	28	.35573	.6	94.8
Q29	1.00000	29	.33114	.6	95.4
Q30	1.00000	30	.30424	.5	95.9
Q31	1.00000	31	.27766	.5	96.4
Q32	1.00000	32	.25916	.5	96.9
Q33	1.00000	33	.23034	.4	97.3
Q34	1.00000	34	.21018	.4	97.6
Q35	1.00000	35	.17409	.3	98.0
Q36	1.00000	36	.14847	.3	98.2
Q37	1.00000	37	.14626	.3	98.5
Q38	1.00000	38	.13547	.2	98.7
Q39	1.00000	39	.11256	.2	98.9
Q40	1.00000	40	.10680	.2	99.1
Q41	1.00000	41	.09334	.2	99.3
Q42	1.00000	42	.08930	.2	99.4
Q43	1.00000	43	.08231	.1	99.6
Q44	1.00000	44	.06777	.1	99.7
Q45	1.00000	45	.05038	.1	99.7
Q46	1.00000	46	.03596	.1	99.8
Q47	1.00000	47	.03232	.1	99.9
Q48	1.00000	48	.03057	.1	99.9
Q49	1.00000	49	.02348	.0	99.9
Q50	1.00000	50	.00919	.0	100.0
Q51	1.00000	51	.00740	.0	100.0

3.2

052	52	1.00000	.00434	.0	100.0
053	53	1.00000	.00145	.0	100.0
054	54	1.00000	.00000	.0	100.0
055	55	1.00000	-.00000	-.0	100.0
056	56	1.00000	-.00000	-.0	100.0
057	57	1.00000	-.00000	-.0	100.0

PRINCIPAL COMPONENTS I   16/08/82   15:07:55.   PAGE   5

FILE   NONAME   (CREATION DATE = 16/08/82)

FACTOR MATRIX USING PRINCIPAL FACTOR, NO ITERATIONS

	FACTOR 1	FACTOR 2	FACTOR 3	FACTOR 4	FACTOR 5	FACTOR 6	FACTOR 7	FACTOR 8	FACTOR 9	FACTOR 10
Q1	.79198	-.00381	.03551	.26497	.08830	-.13969	.08063	-.08248	.00707	.07771
Q2	.67626	.08718	.00298	.11173	-.17418	-.28765	.18117	-.32482	-.12644	-.11776
Q3	.76559	-.21086	.08665	.06078	-.27439	-.08747	.04511	-.07798	.04538	.02538
Q4	.57581	.40036	.00385	.47071	.06455	-.09460	-.05362	.19181	.19396	.24727
Q5	.75070	-.13799	.02360	.10114	.08980	-.02732	-.07732	-.06220	-.11256	.20638
Q6	.69389	-.03543	-.16194	.00986	.24591	.09281	-.01247	.38556	-.21042	.06195
Q7	.72292	-.30357	.01302	-.08783	.03597	-.02147	-.02816	-.00495	-.17867	.19712
Q8	.69337	.03124	.37629	.31676	.12645	.13476	.24697	-.11519	.39521	.24476
Q9	.64562	.15189	.19775	.02199	.23374	-.03564	.21896	-.21612	.03216	.21587
Q10	.80665	-.16716	.03587	.10502	.01933	-.16039	-.01215	-.07166	-.16406	.02234
Q11	.58236	.01057	-.14090	-.41820	-.22763	-.26106	.14376	-.28399	.17196	.09245
Q12	.40760	-.46496	.03110	.14869	.17323	-.16530	.29322	.18426	.00649	.12053
Q13	.55373	-.18740	.04331	.07725	.23968	-.40192	-.00719	.20394	.22640	.09176
Q14	.67570	-.06012	.15847	.26355	-.24613	-.40815	.04590	-.07800	-.07596	-.11076
Q15	.70515	.23146	.18502	.45398	.09284	-.16040	.01584	-.05857	.05277	.05827
Q16	.64348	.39317	.15243	.00789	.01742	-.08101	.24619	-.11563	-.00437	.00127
Q17	.71640	.16464	.21048	.08998	-.03689	-.31872	.05961	.08212	.23509	.06876
Q18	.55370	.52286	.07387	.00278	.11774	-.17592	-.00468	.17706	.18013	.17213
Q19	.69035	-.08706	.30293	-.04056	.27055	-.04738	-.10955	.00014	.25732	.07393
Q20	.42481	-.02418	.36626	.22776	.07475	-.14313	-.13872	-.00443	-.09623	.48908
Q21	.75334	-.04443	.19571	.02106	.17460	-.18123	-.00879	-.02792	.09178	-.06812
Q22	.43636	-.00489	.37627	.51603	.07516	-.00891	.16606	.29507	-.04845	.18576
Q23	.73075	.10149	.29213	.14127	.02783	.05019	-.06479	-.32164	-.14000	.01071
Q24	.54412	.27070	.36614	.01210	.21431	.04930	-.22714	-.02731	-.01372	.28074
Q25	.64186	.49237	.08756	.11783	.06424	.04051	.19487	.03639	.05431	.01970
Q26	.65824	.40489	.29207	.04194	.10982	-.26886	.01450	-.02059	-.04289	.06860
Q27	.64041	.01728	.11706	.03575	.15431	-.15065	-.06115	-.18014	-.03944	.01685
Q28	.58407	.40707	.05240	.24389	.06307	-.10979	-.25566	-.11839	-.01860	.30048
Q29	.68660	.30459	.05825	.01974	.00342	-.09874	-.16723	.04894	.18678	.13701
Q30	.62427	.13148	.13939	.02193	.02565	-.15000	-.33126	-.11294	.15703	.27490
Q31	.76181	.16780	.10462	.21931	.05633	-.09681	-.22267	-.06969	.10477	.17398
Q32	.77762	.15298	.16661	.01939	.11962	-.01294	-.10781	-.13245	-.10579	.18248
Q33	.73263	.24590	.11028	.19030	.38931	-.05933	-.04978	.07649	.09897	.15081
Q34	.54208	.05261	.42633	.00266	.05468	-.12424	-.11832	.25535	.09421	.14607
Q35	.76944	.25003	.07349	.07821	.19395	-.23556	-.23076	-.00895	.07400	.06483
Q36	.50767	.20155	.31407	.09830	.05312	-.24554	.29338	.15598	.48599	.07097
Q37	.57348	.24703	.14332	.21710	.37933	-.05789	-.22512	.36110	.18053	.08522
Q38	.63251	.16891	.20574	.12364	.08291	-.15115	.15011	.06308	.24415	.07786
Q39	.63082	.12747	.32912	.13560	.38563	-.13375	-.08844	.01646	-.16898	.13878
Q40	.65251	.14122	.04296	.29913	.01381	-.04497	.01982	-.10231	.01981	.12522
Q41	.62358	.16667	.18689	.10776	.34107	-.12888	-.27894	.12351	.07785	.39869
Q42	.54217	.18689	.12872	.02354	.14636	-.26094	.12824	-.07726	.32563	.04995
Q43	.47578	.36000	.27645	.02359	.09478	-.18696	-.31697	-.40067	.15750	.01160
Q44	.58285	.35994	.13781	.00581	.28755	-.04021	-.23040	-.14511	.00903	.00093
Q45	.33036	.56432	.37264	.20446	.37456	-.12802	.32312	-.20837	.01579	.01699
Q46	.64235	.27542	.25476	.05523	.03064	-.02334	-.08841	.05613	.19521	.08922
Q47	.65477	.23115	.34824	.27098	.42189	-.26980	-.09918	.03966	.05999	.00476
Q48	.57999	.06674	.15339	.23105		-.34880	-.12690	.07389	.06333	.05380

3.4

049	.55741	-.02181	.22323	.41141	-.13375	.30612	.21613	-.19523	-.15042	.04761
050	.48762	-.10787	-.47114	-.43665	-.08403	.10621	.08960	-.08551	-.06889	-.01917
051	.65467	.08129	-.22632	-.14183	-.26403	-.20446	.26758	.14923	.17964	-.09543
052	.69035	.41694	-.11294	-.18496	.20641	-.03950	-.05449	-.05391	-.01175	-.05469
053	.56679	.03567	-.24268	-.07672	-.22646	-.21310	-.12883	-.06483	-.12886	-.05830
054	.75707	-.40932	-.19731	-.03056	.05676	-.22008	-.33235	-.12004	-.00031	-.03024
055	.58321	-.11179	-.18751	-.07460	-.26201	-.04518	-.07074	-.03084	.10786	.20563
056	.35451	-.05271	-.07354	-.00935	-.08722	-.45830	.20565	.36583	-.39541	-.03930
057	.67910		-.09684	-.33591	-.05243	.13061	-.16967	-.04096	-.02408	-.01896

	FACTOR 11	FACTOR 12	FACTOR 13
Q1	.04177	.24108	-.05075
Q2	-.08620	-.24674	-.08809
Q3	-.01475	.24149	.17356
Q4	-.13983	-.16170	.17426
Q5	-.03422	-.29069	-.05581
Q6	-.01073	.01483	-.14604
Q7	-.21221	.09702	-.07936
Q8	-.22624	.13191	.15026
Q9	-.09591	.17157	-.03623
Q10	.02899	.00052	-.11409
Q11	-.27789	.23121	-.10182
Q12	-.23735	.13134	-.33863
Q13	-.00021	-.27491	.05044
Q14	-.09767	-.05770	-.13330
Q15	-.04725	.06104	-.07926
Q16	.15058	.14972	-.14132
Q17	.01508	-.06270	-.14151
Q18	-.11759	-.05052	.01856
Q19	-.17148	-.04173	.25209
Q20	-.14587	-.11146	-.18865
Q21	-.10405	-.28073	-.01455
Q22	-.12578	.12187	-.11770
Q23	-.13036	.14401	-.07215
Q24	-.29513	-.15283	-.04022
Q25	-.00226	-.12479	-.04866
Q26	-.06200	-.04775	-.27332
Q27		-.13112	-.12089
Q28	-.12486	-.01634	-.09846
Q29	-.29963	-.02291	-.11952
Q30	.14571	-.01490	-.12295
Q31	-.13126	-.16532	-.07617
Q32	-.01990	-.08266	-.08485
Q33	-.11757	-.05257	-.08121
Q34	-.16775	.09003	-.02307
Q35	-.10255	.07455	-.03913
Q36	-.12835	.30228	.26427
Q37	-.12205	.05537	-.13153
Q38	-.02992	-.06331	.13074
Q39	.26920	.20557	-.08393
Q40	-.00389	.19380	-.11030
Q41	-.20417	.10277	-.14964
Q42	.04975	.58085	-.09403
Q43	.02595	.98520	-.27200
Q44	.22111	.55550	-.10823
Q45	.34646	.60742	-.13797
Q46	-.07727	.14260	-.06035
Q47	-.12101	.09044	-.12197
Q48	.04989	.19447	-.10261
Q49	-.13216	.06556	-.23013
Q50	-.18351	.08194	-.01452
Q51	-.10223	-.08514	-.04266

3.6

052	-.00738	.05009	-.11515
053	-.22603	.22478	.26132
054	-.04160	-.19468	-.00967
055	.55255	.01583	-.02711
056	-.22227	.24134	.09768
057	-.15405	-.27175	.23223

FILE   NONAME   (CREATION DATE = 16/08/82)

VARIABLE	COMMUNALITY
Q1	.80563
Q2	.83476
Q3	.81495
Q4	.75558
Q5	.75955
Q6	.79682
Q7	.75580
Q8	.74465
Q9	.71195
Q10	.76294
Q11	.74519
Q12	.84290
Q13	.75022
Q14	.83680
Q15	.84714
Q16	.73699
Q17	.78688
Q18	.74106
Q19	.64593
Q20	.79778
Q21	.75384
Q22	.82508
Q23	.82865
Q24	.75018
Q25	.78411
Q26	.84485
Q27	.83076
Q28	.80213
Q29	.77291
Q30	.70871
Q31	.82431
Q32	.74766
Q33	.72744
Q34	.79229
Q35	.80517
Q36	.87111
Q37	.77435
Q38	.76712
Q39	.74211
Q40	.76501
Q41	.81337
Q42	.74435
Q43	.85564
Q44	.82375
Q45	.76165
Q46	.81481
Q47	.86312
Q48	.79480
Q49	.82517
Q50	.74140
Q51	.77374

3.8

Q52   .76478
Q53   .69651
Q54   .84159

Q55   .68041
Q56   .81252
Q57   .78890

PRINCIPAL COMPONENTS 1

FILE   NONAME   (CREATION DATE = 16/08/82)   16/08/82   15:07:55.   PAGE   8

VARIMAX ROTATED FACTOR MATRIX
AFTER ROTATION WITH KAISER NORMALIZATION

	FACTOR 1	FACTOR 2	FACTOR 3	FACTOR 4	FACTOR 5	FACTOR 6	FACTOR 7	FACTOR 8	FACTOR 9	FACTOR 10
Q1	.42464	.44003	.52737	.27353	.07786	.05004	.15215	-.02307	.13878	.05706
Q2	.21816	.26969	.23319	.29458	.69097	-.00623	.01961	.02656	.02259	-.01157
Q3	.54810	.10933	.30573	.39883	.17657	-.03629	.30646	-.05161	.09733	.21581
Q4	.00286	.28400	.00439	.14756	.07156	.21935	-.02181	.03631	.08532	.17343
Q5	.51044	.51110	.12304	.11733	.40454	.01696	.28132	.24159	.21490	.00632
Q6	.77611	.43985	.15593	.20250	.20216	.26316	.02834	.27257	.21191	-.04886
Q7	.53327	.16223	.32316	.11383	.14234	.10134	.23483	.05324	.38049	-.11679
Q8	.10193	.05781	.15511	.00997	.05142	.11042	.00060	.19551	-.13535	.76263
Q9	.19336	.63207	.22554	.12902	.19248	-.10180	.11822	-.03023	.27992	-.00857
Q10	.59482	.26756	.28534	.23437	.24248	.03892	.07468	.06470	.11382	-.06640
Q11	.14992	.32086	.05707	.33938	.28868	.26416	.50231	-.00560	.07209	-.05940
Q12	.20414	.04016	.11121	.05832	.01498	-.00545	.01385	.08497	.84849	-.00480
Q13	.21424	.25432	.00403	.06013	-.01398	.11146	.08846	.63530	.32694	.21961
Q14	.25505	.09249	.21954	.37116	.00003	.27089	.45256	.38092	.10950	.04924
Q15	.11790	.43308	.68109	.16527	.17912	.21769	.24112	.10025	-.02388	-.03692
Q16	.09762	.66514	.15771	.41500	.18559	.05423	.18697	.07313	.06514	.09259
Q17	.14023	.39050	.22992	.13089	.27355	.28165	.43635	.29171	.18594	.23633
Q18	.03758	.38605	.08998	.22548	.14514	.52403	.26253	.09845	.03325	.09661
Q19	.21763	.07231	.51950	.10955	.10087	.01330	.14412	.37517	-.03631	.27001
Q20	.16890	.02094	.15001	.02091	.11785	.07158	.82289	.08606	.00454	-.03753
Q21	.27049	.20300	.45574	.11364	.38786	.09662	.09822	.34565	.09935	.10114
Q22	.23514	.10166	.00278	.28984	.18493	.40660	.01151	.08320	.31796	.51924
Q23	.47431	.45000	.01664	.28573	.26629	.04401	.05646	-.04221	-.07188	-.10965
Q24	.01476	.06332	.42934	.13557	.38696	.43098	-.02830	.36939	.04657	.14029
Q25	.63369	.16147	.41806	.05278	.10044	.06191	.06134	.16492	.26801	.15460
Q26	.08325	.35360	.47010	.16731	.44030	.46445	.08937	.09598	.00700	.09431
Q27	.45366	.28985	.40905	.17658	.49034	.17986	.17511	.16179	.04961	-.06342
Q28	.27707	.40407	.04371	.01637	.38905	.39158	.17769	.07708	.16111	.08641
Q29	.73746	.20411	.18471	.14325	.07522	.21704	.02692	.03130	.01421	.12326
Q30	.16782	.50984	.05268	.40708	.75974	.11048	.07028	.07065	.16089	.13411
Q31	.49953	.40283	.08973	.02468	.34566	.22495	.07588	.19162	.04761	-.10235
Q32	.54988	.37766	.14653	.20936	.06730	.04379	.20502	.18751	.24544	-.06061
Q33	.52459	.27174	.13967	.15838	.09805	.03347	.11980	.29418	.35822	.09915
Q34	.50227	.20346	.07962	.60929	.07197	.11009	.07930	.08592	.00460	-.13141
Q35	.67907	.15053	.38894	.21990	.19154	.10563	.05947	.10474	.10776	.06973
Q36	.01524	.15500	.15015	.00576	.17300	.09577	.08650	.01984	.02331	.03490
Q37	.58722	.00453	.13471	.11783	.10911	.32298	.08827	.12602	.11810	.29972
Q38	.40442	.40557	.24748	.12736	.08169	.12655	.14887	.23377	.35154	.16622
Q39	.40060	.56549	.00105	.22237	.03184	.14634	.04162	.30181	.17538	-.04176
Q40	.06098	.19783	.01068	.53398	.31730	.21480	.12610	.03982	.00998	.24937
Q41	.02337	.35554	.15956	.67180	.08321	.07898	.09536	.27878	.22445	.15823
Q42	.02880	.66705	.08134	.10817	.06480	.02610	.25737	.39497	.10256	.21872
Q43	.11082	.51551	.15195	.05014	.02751	.86593	.14293	.10528	.01974	.03649
Q44	.94680	.08800	.11433	.01283	.10808	.05656	.08692	.06587	.06607	.12818
Q45	.16446	.69601	.10495	.08692	.05010	.21341	.23140	.04914	.23465	.63730
Q46	.30778	.73310	.23074	.04076	.05087	.22246	-.07559	.05198	.092A3	-.0601A
Q47	.40791	.02402	.69964	.15291	.07204	-.01529	.25850	.03097	.19518	.07041

Q48	.29168	.45791	.67528	-.11229	-.05556	.14911	-.02574	-.02591	.06935	.07851
Q49	.19221	.13740	-.10142	.10795	.53427	.22844	.18305	.06947	.44615	.27886
Q50	.14683	.07501	.49711	.06073	.05629	.13407	.55109	.05432	.00100	.24077

FILE NONAME   (CREATION DATE = 20/09/82)

- - - - - - - - - - - - - - - -   D I S C R I M I N A N T   A N A L Y S I S   - - - - - - - - - - - - - - -

ON GROUPS DEFINED BY GROUP

ANALYSIS NUMBER   1

DIRECT METHOD- ALL VARIABLES PASSING THE TOLERANCE TEST ARE ENTERED.

    MINIMUM TOLERANCE LEVEL.................   .00100

CANONICAL DISCRIMINANT FUNCTIONS

    MAXIMUM NUMBER OF FUNCTIONS.............   2
    MINIMUM CUMULATIVE PERCENT OF VARIANCE.... 100.00
    MAXIMUM SIGNIFICANCE OF WILKS LAMBDA.....   1.0000

PRIOR PROBABILITY FOR EACH GROUP IS .50000

CANONICAL DISCRIMINANT FUNCTIONS

		PERCENT OF	CUMULATIVE	CANONICAL	AFTER FUNCTION	WILKS LAMBDA	CHI-SQUARED	D.F.	SIGNIFICANCE
FUNCTION	EIGENVALUE	VARIANCE	PERCENT	CORRELATION					
					0	.7856739	11.581	18	.8681
1*	.19042	73.59	73.59	.3994482	1	.9352204	3.2147	10	.9759
2*	.04595	15.30	82.89	.2181075	2	.9819318	.87521	4	.9281
3	.01640	7.11	100.00	.1344181					

    * MARKS THE 2 FUNCTION(S) TO BE USED IN THE REMAINING ANALYSIS.

STANDARDIZED CANONICAL DISCRIMINANT FUNCTION COEFFICIENTS

	FUNC 1	FUNC 2
FACT1	-.16503	.02104
FACT2	-.94034	.17610
FACT3	-.04054	-.93332
FACT4	1.03781	-.33705
FACT5	-.22124	-.32492
FACT6	-.50514	.47656

CANONICAL DISCRIMINANT FUNCTIONS EVALUATED AT GROUP MEANS (GROUP CENTROIDS)

GROUP	FUNC 1	FUNC 2
1	-.46227	.10016
2	.47121	.15475

3   -.28336   -.15722
4   .24787   -.45303

DISCRIMINANT ANALYSIS FIVE   28/09/82   16.24.23.   PAGE   6

CPU TIME REQUIRED..   .7160 SECONDS

        DISCRIMINANT   GROUPS=GROUP(1,2)/VARIABLES=FACT1 TO FACT6/
                        ANALYSIS=FACT1 TO FACT6/
                        FUNCTIONS=2/

00074700 CM REQUIRED FOR DISCRIMINANT ANALYSIS

    OPTION - 1
    IGNORE MISSING VALUE INDICATORS
    (NO MISSING VALUES DEFINED...OPTION 1 WAS FORCED)

DISCRIMINANT ANALYSIS FIVE   28/09/82   16.55.23.   PAGE   5

FILE   NONAME   (CREATION DATE = 28/09/82)

- - - - - - - - - - - - - - - - - D I S C R I M I N A N T   A N A L Y S I S - - - - - - - - - - - - - - - -

ON GROUPS DEFINED BY GROUP

ANALYSIS NUMBER   1

DIRECT METHOD- ALL VARIABLES PASSING THE TOLERANCE TEST ARE ENTERED.

    MINIMUM TOLERANCE LEVEL.....................   .00100

CANONICAL DISCRIMINANT FUNCTIONS

    MAXIMUM NUMBER OF FUNCTIONS.............   1
    MINIMUM CUMULATIVE PERCENT OF VARIANCE... 100.00
    MAXIMUM SIGNIFICANCE OF WILKS LAMBDA.....   1.0000

PRIOR PROBABILITY FOR EACH GROUP IS .10000

THE FOLLOWING 1 VARIABLES FAILED THE TOLERANCE TEST..

              WITHIN   MINIMUM
              GROUPS
VARIABLE   VARIANCE   TOLERANCE   TOLERANCE
  O5   2.42500   .0000000   .0000000

                              CANONICAL DISCRIMINANT FUNCTIONS

                    PERCENT OF   CUMULATIVE   CANONICAL   - AFTER
FUNCTION EIGENVALUE VARIANCE   PERCENT   CORRELATION - FUNCTION WILKS LAMBDA   CHI-SQUARED   D.F.   SIGNIFICANCE
                                                           :   0   .8134773   2.4780   4   .6486
   1*   .22937   100.00   100.00   .4319606   :

    * MARKS THE   1 FUNCTION(S) TO BE USED IN THE REMAINING ANALYSIS.

STANDARDIZED CANONICAL DISCRIMINANT FUNCTION COEFFICIENTS

              FUNC 1

   O1   .52397
   O2   .65641
   O3   .91504
   O4   1.19443

UNSTANDARDIZED CANONICAL DISCRIMINANT FUNCTION COEFFICIENTS

4.4

FUNC 1

	FUNC 1
D1	.44PC155
D2	.45C7217
D3	.5756467
D4	.8727393
(CONSTANT)	-7.15P039

CANCNICAL DISCRIMINANT FUNCTIONS EVALUATED AT GROUP MEANS (GROUP CENTROIDS)

GROUP	FUNC 1
3	-.44795
4	.44795

4.5

DISCRIMINANT ANALYSIS PAGE

FILE NONAME (CREATION DATE = 28/09/82)

- - - - - - - - - - - - - - - D I S C R I M I N A N T   A N A L Y S I S - - - - - - - - - - - - - - -

ON GROUPS DEFINED BY GROUP

ANALYSIS NUMBER   1

DIRECT METHOD- ALL VARIABLES PASSING THE TOLERANCE TEST ARE ENTERED.

MINIMUM TOLERANCE LEVEL.................   .00100

CANONICAL DISCRIMINANT FUNCTIONS

MAXIMUM NUMBER OF FUNCTIONS.............   1
MINIMUM CUMULATIVE PERCENT OF VARIANCE...   100.00
MAXIMUM SIGNIFICANCE OF WILKS LAMBDA.....   1.0000

PRIOR PROBABILITY FOR EACH GROUP IS .50000

THE FOLLOWING   1 VARIABLES FAILED THE TOLERANCE TEST..

	WITHIN GROUPS VARIANCE	TOLERANCE	MINIMUM TOLERANCE
VARIABLE			
D5	1.45904	.0000000	.0000000

CANONICAL DISCRIMINANT FUNCTIONS

FUNCTION	EIGENVALUE	PERCENT OF VARIANCE	CUMULATIVE PERCENT	CANONICAL CORRELATION	AFTER FUNCTION	WILKS LAMBDA	CHI-SQUARED	D.F.	SIGNIFICANCE
					0	.8745658	4.5569	4	.3358
1*	.14342	100.00	100.00	.3541669					

* MARKS THE   1 FUNCTION(S) TO BE USED IN THE REMAINING ANALYSIS.

STANDARDIZED CANONICAL DISCRIMINANT FUNCTION COEFFICIENTS

FUNC 1

D1	-.56035
D2	-.98772
D3	-.57498
D4	.05735

UNSTANDARDIZED CANONICAL DISCRIMINANT FUNCTION COEFFICIENTS

4.6

FUNC 1

D1   -.446F023
D2   -.757R081
D3   -.329S022
D4   .3945R46E-01
(CONSTANT) 5.076063

CANONICAL DISCRIMINANT FUNCTIONS EVALUATED AT GROUP MEANS (GROUP CENTROIDS)

GROUP   FUNC 1

1   .36861
2   -.36861

```
26 GROUPS AFTER COMBINING G 19 (N= 1) AND G 25 (N= 1), ERROR =  31.5000000000
25 GROUPS AFTER COMBINING G  4 (N= 2) AND G 32 (N= 1), ERROR =  32.1666666667
24 GROUPS AFTER COMBINING G  2 (N= 3) AND G 42 (N= 2), ERROR =  32.7000000000
23 GROUPS AFTER COMBINING G  4 (N= 4) AND G 24 (N= 3), ERROR =  34.6190476190
22 GROUPS AFTER COMBINING G  1 (N= 1) AND G 20 (N= 1), ERROR =  35.5000000000
21 GROUPS AFTER COMBINING G  4 (N= 1) AND G 51 (N= 1), ERROR =  35.5000000000
20 GROUPS AFTER COMBINING G  4 (N= 3) AND G 16 (N= 1), ERROR =  36.3333333333
19 GROUPS AFTER COMBINING G  7 (N= 1) AND G 27 (N= 4), ERROR =  37.7500000000
18 GROUPS AFTER COMBINING G  2 (N= 5) AND G  3 (N= 4), ERROR =  37.9388888889
17 GROUPS AFTER COMBINING G  4 (N= 4) AND G 10 (N= 1), ERROR =  38.6500000000
16 GROUPS AFTER COMBINING G  5 (N= 1) AND G 28 (N= 1), ERROR =  41.0000000000
15 GROUPS AFTER COMBINING G  1 (N= 2) AND G  7 (N= 5), ERROR =  41.9285714286
14 GROUPS AFTER COMBINING G  2 (N= 9) AND G 22 (N= 3), ERROR =  42.6111111111
13 GROUPS AFTER COMBINING G  5 (N= 5) AND G 17 (N= 6), ERROR =  44.2515151515
12 GROUPS AFTER COMBINING G  6 (N= 2) AND G 18 (N= 1), ERROR =  45.8333333333
11 GROUPS AFTER COMBINING G  5 (N= 2) AND G 13 (N= 2), ERROR =  55.5000000000
10 GROUPS AFTER COMBINING G  2 (N=12) AND G  6 (N= 3), ERROR =  55.8333333333
 9 GROUPS AFTER COMBINING G  4 (N=11) AND G 12 (N= 2), ERROR =  62.2587412587
 8 GROUPS AFTER COMBINING G  1 (N= 7) AND G  8 (N=13), ERROR =  69.9445054945
 7 GROUPS AFTER COMBINING G  4 (N= 4) AND G 50 (N= 1), ERROR =  71.0000000000
 6 GROUPS AFTER COMBINING G  2 (N=15) AND G  9 (N= 7), ERROR =  73.2748917749
 5 GROUPS AFTER COMBINING G  2 (N=22) AND G 10 (N= 2), ERROR =  76.8093939394

 4 GROUPS AFTER COMBINING G  4 (N= 5) AND G  5 (N= 4), ERROR =  82.0555555555
G  1 (N= 20) 101 107 108 110 112 115 117 121 122 124 128 131 137 140 141
             143 149 152 156 158
G  2 (N= 24) 102 103 106 109 111 119 123 125 126 127 130 136 138 139
             142 146 147 148 150 151 153 155 157 154
G  4 (N=  9) 104 105 113 114 116 129 133 135
G 31 (N=  1) 132

 3 GROUPS AFTER COMBINING G  2 (N= 24) AND G 31 (N= 1), ERROR =  91.3433333333
G  1 (N= 20) 101 107 108 110 112 115 117 121 122 124 128 131 137 140 141
             143 149 152 156 158
G  2 (N= 25) 102 103 106 109 111 118 119 123 125 126 127 130 132 136 138
             139 142 146 147 148 150 151 153 155 157
G  4 (N=  9) 104 105 113 114 116 129 133 135

 2 GROUPS AFTER COMBINING G  1 (N= 20) AND G  2 (N= 25), ERROR = 129.1233333332
```

5.2

```
G  1 (N= 45)  101  102  103  106  107  108  109  110  111  112  115  117  118  119  121
              122  123  124  125  126  127  128  130  131  132  136  137  138  139  140
              141  142  143  146  147  148  149  150  151  152  153  155  156  157  158
G  4 (N= 9)   104  105  113  114  116  129  133  135  154

END-OF-FILE ENCOUNTERED: FILENAME =  INPUT
ERROR NUMBER  65  DETECTED BY INPC =  AT ADDRESS  000152
CALLED FROM CCDS  AT  LINE 13
CALLED FROM HGROUP AT  LINE 28
```

FILE   NONAME   (CREATION DATE = 14/09/82)

-   D I S C R I M I N A N T   A N A L Y S I S   -

ON GROUPS DEFINED BY GROUP

ANALYSIS NUMBER   1

DIRECT METHOD- ALL VARIABLES PASSING THE TOLERANCE TEST ARE ENTERED.

MINIMUM TOLERANCE LEVEL................ .00100

CANONICAL DISCRIMINANT FUNCTION

MAXIMUM NUMBER OF FUNCTIONS............... 1
MINIMUM CUMULATIVE PERCENT OF VARIANCE... 100.00
MAXIMUM SIGNIFICANCE OF WILKS LAMBDA..... 1.0000

PRIOR PROBABILITY FOR EACH GROUP IS   .50000

THE FOLLOWING   1 VARIABLES FAILED THE TOLERANCE TEST..

	WITHIN GROUPS VARIANCE	TOLERANCE	MINIMUM TOLERANCE
VARIABLE			
COPE6	2.18129	.0000000	.0000000

CANONICAL DISCRIMINANT FUNCTIONS

FUNCTION	EIGENVALUE	PERCENT OF VARIANCE	CUMULATIVE PERCENT	CANONICAL CORRELATION	AFTER FUNCTION	WILKS LAMBDA	CHI-SQUARED	D.F.	SIGNICANCE
					0	.5991060	17.163	5	.0042
1*	.66915	100.00	100.00	.6331619					

* MARKS THE   1 FUNCTION(S) TO BE USED IN THE REMAINING ANALYSIS.

STANDARDIZED CANONICAL DISCRIMINANT FUNCTION COEFFICIENTS

	FUNC 1
COPE1	.71893
COPE2	-.35434
COPE3	-.05895
COPE4	-.69771
COPE5	-.92734

CANONICAL DISCRIMINANT FUNCTIONS EVALUATED AT GROUP MEANS (GROUP CENTROIDS)

6.2

GROUP	FUNC 1
1	.79620
2	-.79620

www.ingramcontent.com/pod-product-compliance
Lightning Source LLC
Chambersburg PA
CBHW080251200326
41519CB00023B/6953